Tipping recommendations

The figures below are shown either as a percentage of the bill or in escudos or cruzeiros. They indicate a s̶ ̶ ̶ ̶ ̶ ̶ for the service described Wh̶ ̶ ̶ ̶ ̶ ̶ ̶ ̶ ̶ ̶ ̶ted and the percentage ̶ ̶ ̶ ̶ ̶ ̶ ̶ ̶ ffi-cially discouraged, t̶ ̶ ̶ ̶ ̶ ̶ ̶ ̶rs and taxi drivers. Eve̶ ̶ ̶ ̶ ̶ ̶ps are sometimes expec̶ ̶ ̶ ̶ ̶ ̶n-ary to round off a pa̶ ̶ ̶ ̶

Note: Inflation in B̶ ̶ ̶ ̶ ̶ ̶ampant that the figures in cruzeiros be̶ ̶ ̶ will soon be outdated. To avoid embarrassment, ask for local advice.

	Portugal	Brazil
HOTEL		
Service charge, bill	10–15% (incl.)	10% (gen. incl.)
Porter, per bag	20 esc.	Cr$ 500
Bellboy, errand	20 esc.	Cr$ 500
Maid (per week)	200 esc. (optional)	Cr$ 5,000
Doorman, hails cab	20 esc.	Cr$ 300–500
RESTAURANT		
Service charge, bill	15% (incl.)	10% (gen. incl.)
Waiter	5–10% (optional)	5–10%
Hat check	10–15 esc.	Cr$ 200
Lavatory attendant	10 esc.	Cr$ 100
Taxi driver	10%	round up
Hairdresser/Barber	10%	10%
Theatre/		
Cinema usher	10 esc.	none
Tour guide	10–15%	Cr$ 2,000–3,000
Filling-station		
attendant	10 esc.	Cr$ 200

BERLITZ PHRASE BOOKS

World's bestselling phrase books feature not only expressions and vocabulary you'll need, but also travel tips, useful facts and pronunciation throughout. The handiest and most readable conversation aid available.

Arabic	French	Portuguese
Chinese	German	Russian
Danish	Greek	Serbo-Croatian
Dutch	Hebrew	Spanish
European	Hungarian	Latin-American
(14 languages)	Italian	Spanish
European	Japanese	Swahili
Menu Reader	Norwegian	Swedish
Finnish	Polish	Turkish

BERLITZ CASSETTEPAKS

The above-mentioned titles are also available combined with a cassette to help you improve your accent. A helpful 32-page script is included containing the complete text of the dual language hi-fi recording.

PORTUGUESE
FOR TRAVELLERS

By the staff of Editions Berlitz

Library of Congress Catalog Card Number: 75-11285

Revised edition
14th printing 1986

Printed in Switzerland

Editions Berlitz
1, avenue des Jordils
1000 Lausanne 6, Switzerland

Preface

In preparing this complete revision of *Portuguese for Travellers,* we took into consideration a wealth of suggestions received from phrase-book users around the world. As a result, this new edition features:

a) a complete phonetic transcription throughout indicating the pronunciation of all words and phrases you'll need to know on your trip

b) special sections showing the replies your listener might give to you. Just hand him the book and let him point to the appropriate phrase. This is especially practical in difficult situations (doctor, garage mechanic, etc.)

c) more consideration to the Brazilian usage of Portuguese: the Brazilian alternatives are given in brackets [ ]

d) a tipping chart and a more comprehensive reference section in the back of the book.

These new features complement what has become the world's most popular phrase-book series, helping you with:

* all the phrases and supplementary vocabulary you'll need on your trip

* a wide variety of tourist and travel facts, tips and useful information, primarily for Portugal, but also covering many aspects of travel in Brazil

* a logical system of presentation so that you can find the right phrase for the immediate situation

* quick reference through colour coding. The major features of the contents are on the back cover. A complete index is found inside.

These are just a few of the practical advantages. In addition, the book will prove a valuable introduction to life in Portugal and Brazil.

A comprehensive section on Eating Out gives you translations and explanations for practically anything one would find on a Portuguese menu; there's a complete Shopping Guide that enables you to obtain virtually anything you want. Trouble with the car? Turn to the mechanic's manual with its dual-language terms. Feeling ill? Our medical section provides the most rapid communication possible between you and the doctor.

To make the most of *Portuguese for Travellers,* we suggest that you start with the "Guide to Pronunciation". Then go on to "Some Basic Expressions". This not only gives you a minimum vocabulary, it helps you to pronounce the language.

We are particularly grateful to Mrs. Maria Helena da Cruz-Pinto, Mrs. Joanne Weil and Mr. António Costa for their help in the preparation of this book and to Dr. T.J.A. Bennett who devised the phonetic transcription. We also wish to thank the Portuguese National Tourist Office for its assistance.

We shall be very pleased to receive any comments, criticisms and suggestions that you think may help us in preparing future editions.

Thank you. Have a good trip.

Throughout this book, the symbols illustrated here indicate small sections where phrases have been compiled that your foreign listener might like to say to *you.* If you don't understand him, give him the book and let him point to the phrase in his language. The English translation is just beside it.

A very basic grammar

Here's the briefest possible outline of some essential features of Portuguese grammar.

Articles

Articles agree in gender and number with the noun.

Definite article (the):

	masculine	feminine
singular	**o**	**a**
plural	**os**	**as**

Indefinite article (a/an):

	masculine	feminine
singular	**um**	**uma**
plural	**uns**	**umas**

Note: The plural corresponds to the English "some" or "a few".

To show possession, the preposition **de** (of) + the article is contracted to **do, da, dos** or **das.**

o princípio do mês	the beginning of the month
o fim da semana	the end of the week

Nouns

All nouns in Portuguese are either masculine or feminine. Normally, those ending in **o** are masculine and those ending in **a** are feminine. Generally, nouns which end in a vowel add **-s** to form the plural:

a menina	the little girl
as meninas	the little girls
o galo	the cock
os galos	the cocks

Words ending in **r, s** or **z** form the plural by adding **-es:**

a mulher	the woman
as mulheres	the women
o país	the country
os países	the countries
a luz	the light
as luzes	the lights

Words ending in a nasal sound **(em, im, om, um)** change their endings to **ens, ins, ons, uns** in the plural.

Adjectives

They agree with the nouns they modify in gender and number.

o belo livro	the nice book
a bela estátua	the fine statue
os homens altos	the tall men
as mulheres altas	the tall women

From these examples you can see that adjectives can come before or after the noun. This is a matter of sound and idiom.

Demonstrative adjectives

this	**este** (masc.)/**esta** (fem.)
that	**esse, aquele** (masc.)/ **essa, aquela** (fem.)
these	**estes** (masc.)/**estas** (fem.)
those	**esses, aqueles** (masc.)/ **essas, aquelas** (fem.)

The difference between the three forms is that **este** means within reach, **esse** a bit farther and **aquele** means out of reach. There are also three invariable demonstrative adjectives in Portuguese: **isto, isso** and **aquilo.**

Tome isto.	Take this.
Deixe isso, por favor.	Leave that, please.
Dê-me aquilo, ali.	Give me that, there.

Possessive adjectives

These agree in number and gender with the noun they modify, i.e., with the thing possessed and not the possessor.

	masculine	feminine
my	meu	minha
your	teu	tua
his/her/its	seu	sua
our	nosso	nossa
your	vosso	vossa
their	seu	sua

All these forms add an **s** to form the plural.

Note: The form of the third person can be used instead of the second, as a form of politeness:

Meu amigo, o seu livro deixou-me óptima impressão.	My friend, your book made a very good impression on me.

Personal pronouns

	subject	direct object	indirect object
I	eu	me	mim
you	tu	te	ti
he/it	ele	o	lhe
she/it	ela	a	lhe
we	nós	nos	nos
you	vós	vos	vos
they (masc.)	eles	os	lhes
they (fem.)	elas	as	lhes

There are two forms for "you" (singular) in Portuguese: the intimate **tu** when talking to relatives, friends and children and **você,** which is used in all other cases between people not knowing each other very well. But when addressing someone you normally use the third person of the singular or of the plural (this is the polite form used throughout this book):

Como está (estão)?	How are you?

Verbs

There are four auxiliary verbs in Portuguese:

ter/haver	to have
ser/estar	to be

Ter indicates possession or a condition:

Tenho uma casa.	I have a house.
Tenho febre.	I have a fever.

Haver in the meaning of "to exist" is only used in the third person of the singular:

Há muitas pessoas aqui.	There are too many people here.

Ser indicates a permanent state:

Sou inglês.	I am English.

Estar indicates movement or non-permanent state:

Estou a passear.	I am walking.
Está doente.	He is ill.

	ter (to have)	ser (to be)	estar (to be)
eu	tenho	sou	estou
tu	tens	és	estás
ele/ela	tem	é	está
nós	temos	somos	estamos
vós	tendes	sois	estais
eles	têm	são	estão

Normally, the Portuguese do not use personal pronouns since the form of the verb and the sense of the phrase indicate the person:

Tens sede?	Are you thirsty?
Do que está a falar?	What is he/she talking about?

The three conjugations for regular verbs are distinguished by the ending of the infinitive.

	falar (to speak)	viver (to live)	partir (to leave)
eu	falo	vivo	parto
tu	falas	vives	partes
ele/ela	fala	vive	parte
nós	falamos	vivemos	partimos
vós	falais	viveis	partis
eles	falam	vivem	partem

As in all languages, the irregular verbs have to be learned. Here are four you'll find useful:

	poder (to be able)	dizer (to say)	ir (to go)	pedir (to ask)
eu	posso	digo	vou	peço
tu	podes	dizes	vais	pedes
ele/ela	pode	diz	vai	pede
nós	podemos	dizemos	vamos	pedimos
vós	podeis	dizeis	ides	pedis
eles	podem	dizem	vão	pedem

The **negative** is formed by placing **não** before the verb.

Falo português.	I speak Portuguese.
Não falo português.	I don't speak Portuguese.

In Portuguese, **questions** are often formed by changing the intonation of your voice. Very often the personal pronoun is left out both in affirmative sentences and in questions.

Está bem.	It's all right.
Está bem?	Is it all right?
Falo inglês.	I speak English.
Fala inglês?	Do you speak English?

GRAMMAR

Guide to pronunciation

This and the following chapter are intended to make you familiar with the phonetic transcription we've devised and to help you get used to the sounds of Portuguese.

As a minimum vocabulary for your trip, we've selected a number of basic words and phrases under the title "Some Basic Expressions" (pages 17—21).

An outline of the spelling and sounds of Portuguese

The imitated pronunciation used in this book should be read as if it were English except for any special rules set out below. It is based on Standard British pronunciation, though we have tried to take account of General American pronunciation also. Of course, the sounds of any two languages are never exactly the same; but if you follow carefully the indications supplied here, you should be able to read our transcriptions in such a way as to make yourself understood.

Letters written in **bold** should be read with more stress (louder) than the others.

Consonants

Letter	Approximate pronunciation	Symbol	Example	
f, k, l, p, t, v	as in English			
b	as in English, but often less decisive (more like **v**)	b bh	**boca** **abrir**	**bo**aker erbh**reer**
c	1) before **a, o, u**, or a consonant, like **k** in kill	k	**casa**	**kah**zer
	2) before **e** and **i**, like **s** in sit	s	**cedo**	**say**dhoo
ç	like **s** in sit	s	**começar**	koomer**ssahr**

PRONUNCIATION

ch	like **sh** in **sh**ut	sh	**chamar**	sher**mahr**
d	as in English, but often less decisive, especially between vowels (more like **th** in **th**is)	d dh	**dia** **cedo**	**dee**er **say**dhoo
g	1) before **a**, **o** and **u** or a consonant, or after **l**, **n** and **r**, like **g** in **g**o	g/gh	**garfo** **guia**	**gahr**foo **ghee**er
	2) between vowels, like a soft version of the **ch** in Scottish lo**ch**	g	**rogar**	roo**gahr**
	3) before **e** and **i**, like **s** in pleasure	zh	**gelo**	**zhay**loo
h	always silent		**homem**	**om**mayng
j	like **s** in plea**s**ure	zh	**já**	zhah
lh	like **lli** in mi**lli**on	ly	**olho**	**oal**yoo
m	1) between a vowel and a consonant, or at the end of a word ("finally"), it indicates that the vowel is nasalized (see "Nasal vowels")		**embalar** **bom**	ahng^{y}bah**lahr** bawng
	2) elsewhere like **m** in met	m	**mais**	mighsh
n	1) when initial or between vowels, like **n** in **n**o	n	**novo**	**noa**voo
	2) in a consonant group and in plural endings it nasalizes the preceding vowel, but is generally silent		**branco** **homens**	**brahng**koo **om**mahng^{y}sh
nh	like **ni** in o**ni**on	ny	**vinho**	**vee**nyoo
q	like **k** in **k**ill	k	**quadro**	**kwah**droo
r	strongly trilled as in Scottish speech	r	**rua**	**roo**er
s	1) when initial, after a consonant or written **ss**, like **s** in **s**it	s/ss	**saber**	ser**bayr**
	2) between vowels (not necessarily in the same word), like **z** in ra**z**or	z	**casa** **as aves**	**kah**zer erzh **ah**versh
	3) when final, or before **c, f, p, q, t**, like **sh** in **sh**ut	sh	**país**	per**eesh**
	4) elsewhere, like **s** in pleasure	zh	**cisne**	**seezh**ner

x	1) generally like **sh** in **sh**ut	sh	**baixo**	**bigh**shoo
	2) in **ex-** before a vowel, like **z** in ra**z**or	z	**exacto**	i**zz**ahtoo
	3) sometimes like **x** in e**x**it	ks	**táxi**	**tah**ksi
z	1) when initial or between vowels like **z** in ra**z**or	z	**zero**	**z**ehroo
	2) when final or before **c, f, p, q, s** or **t**, like **sh** in **sh**ut	sh	**feliz**	fer**leesh**
	3) elsewhere like **s** in plea**s**ure	zh	**luz da**	**loozh** der

Vowels

a	1) like a mixture of the **u** in c**u**t and the **ar** in p**ar**ty	ah	**nado**	**nah**dhoo
	2) when unstressed or before **m, n** or **nh,** but not in the same syllable, like **a** in **a**bout	er*	**porta**	**por**ter
e	1) when stressed generally like **e** in g**e**t	eh	**perto**	**peh**rtoo
	2) when stressed sometimes like **a** in l**a**te	ay	**cabelo**	ker**b**hayloo
	3) when unstressed, like **er** in oth**er**	er*	**pesado**	per**z**ahdhoo
	4) at the beginning of a word and in certain other cases, like **i** in h**i**t	i	**exacto** **antes**	**i**zzahtoo **ahng**tersh
é	like **e** in g**e**t	eh	**café**	ker**feh**
ê	like **a** in l**a**te, but a pure vowel, not a diphthong	ay	**mês**	maysh
i	1) when stressed like **ee** in s**ee**d	ee	**riso**	**ree**zoo
	2) when unstressed, like **i** in com**i**ng	i	**final**	**fi**nnahl
o	1) when stressed, like **o** in r**o**d	o	**fora**	**fo**rrer
	2) sometimes when stressed or unstressed, like **o** in n**o**te (most common **o**-sound)	oa	**voltar** **Lisboa**	vo**al**tahr li**zh**bhoaer
	3) when unstressed, usually like **oo** in f**oo**t	oo	**caso**	**kah**zoo

---

* The r should not be pronounced when reading this transcription.

ô, ou	like o in note	oa	pôs	poash
u	1) generally like oo in soon	oo	número	noomerroo
	2) silent in gu and qu before e or i		querer	kerrayr

Diphthongs

A diphthong is two vowels pronounced as a single vowel sound, e.g., in English **boy** there is a diphthong consisting of **o** plus a weak **i** sound. In Portuguese diphthongs, **a, e** and **o** are strong vowels and **i** and **u** are weak vowels. In diphthongs the strong vowels are pronounced with more emphasis than the weak ones, e.g., **ai** is pronounced like **igh** in s**igh**, and **au** like **ow** in h**ow**. Sometimes the weak vowels can combine to make a diphthong. Apart from these generalizations the exact pronunciation of Portuguese diphthongs is not easy to predict.

Nasal vowels

These are pronounced through the mouth and through the nose at the same time, just as in the French nasal vowels (e.g., in the French b**on**) and quite similar to the nasal twang heard in some areas of America and Britain.

ã, am, an	something like ung in lung, or like an in French dans	ahng	maçã	merssahng
em, en	something like ing in sing, but recalling also the a in late	ayng	cento	sayngtoo
im, in	a nasalized version of the ea in learn	eeng	cinco	seengkoo
om, on	like orn in corncob or like on in French bon	awng	bom	bawng
um, un	something like a North of England pronunciation of ung in lung (a nasalized version of u in put)	oong	um	oong

PRONUNCIATION

Semi-nasalized diphthongs

In these, the first element is nasalized and combined with a weak **i** (pronounced like y in yet) or **u** (pronounced like w in was).

ăe, ăi, êm, final **en**, usually final **em**	pronounced as **ă** followed by **y** in yet	ahng^y	**mãe** mahng^y **sem** sahng^y
ão, final unstressed **am**	pronounced as **ă** followed by **w** in was	ahng^w	**mão** mahng^w
ŏe, oi	pronounced as **orn** in **corn**-cob or as **on** in French **bon**, followed by **y** in yet	awng^y	**põe** pawng^y
ui	like nasal vowel **u** followed by **y** in yet	oong^y	**muito** moong^{y}too

Stress

1) If a word ends with **a, e** or **o,** the stress falls on the next to the last syllable, e.g., **rosa** (pronounced **ro**zzer). Plural endings **m** and **s** are generally disregarded.
2) All other words are stressed on the las̄   lable, e.g., **animal** (pronounced erni**mmah**l).
3) Words not stressed in accordance with these rules have an accent (´ or `) over the vowel of the stressed syllable.

Brazilian Portuguese

Brazilian Portuguese differs from the Portuguese spoken in Portugal in several important respects. The Brazilian pronunciation is slower and the words are less linked together than in Portugal. Unstressed vowels sound clearer when spoken by Brazilians, while in Portugal they're rapidly slurred over; s‘and z at the end of a syllable tend to be pronounced like s in sit and z in razor (rather than like **sh** in s**h**ut or s in pleasure). Vowel groups or diphthongs are often simplified.

Some basic expressions

Yes.	**Sim.**	seeng
No.	**Não.**	nahng^w
Please.	**Por favor.**	poor fer**voar**
Thank you.	**Obrigado.**	oobrig**gah**dhoo
Thank you very much.	**Muito obrigado.**	**moong**^ytoo oobrig**gah**dhoo
That's all right.	**Não tem de quê.**	nahng^w tayng der kay

Greetings

Good morning.	**Bom dia.**	bawng **dee**er
Good afternoon.	**Boa tarde.**	boaer **tahr**der
Good evening.	**Boa noite.**	boaer **nawng**^yter
Good night.	**Boa noite.**	boaer **nawng**^yter
Good-bye.	**Adeus.**	erd**he**hoosh
See you later.	**Até logo.**	er**teh** loggoo
This is Mr...	**Apresento-lhe o Senhor...**	erprer**zayng**too lyer oo sernyoar
This is Mrs...	**Apresento-lhe a Senhora...**	erprer**zayng**too lyer er sernyorrer
This is Miss...	**Apresento-lhe a Menina...**	erprer**zayng**too lyer er mernee**ener**
I'm very pleased to meet you.	**Muito prazer em conhecê-lo.**	**moong**^ytoo prer**zayr** ayng koonyer**ssay** loo
How are you?	**Como está?**	**koa**moo ish**tah**
Very well, thank you.	**Muito bem, obrigado.**	**moong**^ytoo bayng oobrig**gah**dhoo
And you?	**E você?**	ee vos**say**
Fine.	**Bem.**	bayng
Excuse me.	**Desculpe.**	dersh**kool**per

Questions

Where?	Onde?	awngder
Where's...?	Onde está...?	awngder ishtah
Where are...?	Onde estão...?	awngder ishtahng^w
When?	Quando?	kwahngdoo
What?	O quê?	oo kay
How?	Como?	koamoo
How much?	Quanto?	kwahngtoo
How many?	Quantos?	kwahngtoosh
Who?	Quem?	kayng
Why?	Porquê?	poorkay
Which?	Qual?	kwahl
What do you call this?	Como se chama isto?	koamoo ser shahmer ishtoo
What do you call that?	Como se chama aquilo?	koamoo ser shahmer erkeeloo
What does this mean?	Que significa isto?	ker signiffeeker ishtoo
What does that mean?	Que significa aquilo?	ker signiffeeker erkeeloo

Do you speak...?

Do you speak English?	Fala inglês?	fahler eengglaysh
Do you speak German?	Fala alemão?	fahler erlermahng^w
Do you speak French?	Fala francês?	fahler frahngsaysh
Do you speak Spanish?	Fala espanhol?	fahler ishpernyoll
Do you speak Italian?	Fala italiano?	fahler itterlyahnoo
Could you speak more slowly, please?	Pode falar mais devagar, por favor?	podher ferlahr mighsh dervergahr poor fervoar
Please point to the phrase in the book.	Por favor, indique-me a frase no livro.	poor fervoar eengdeeker mer er frahzer noo leevroo

Just a minute, please. I'll see if I can find it in this book.	**Um momento por favor, vou ver se posso encontrá-la neste livro.**	oong moo**mayng**too poor fervoar voa vayr ser **possoo** ayng**kawng**trah ler **nay**shter **lee**vroo
I understand.	**Compreendo.***	kawngprer**ayng**dhoo
I don't understand.	**Não compreendo.***	nahng^w kawngprer**ayng**dhoo

Can...?

Can I have...?	**Pode dar-me...?**	**po**dher dahr mer
Can we have...?	**Pode dar-nos...?**	**po**dher dahr noosh
Can you show me...?	**Pode mostrar--me...?**	**po**dher moosh**trahr** mer
Can you tell me...?	**Pode dizer-me...?**	**po**dher di**zzayr** mer
Can you help me, please?	**Pode ajudar-me, por favor?**	**po**dher erzhood**hahr** mer poor fer**voar**

Wanting

I'd like...	**Queria...**	ker**ree**er
We'd like...	**Queríamos...**	ker**ree**ermoosh
Please give me...	**Por favor, dê-me...**	poor fer**voar** day mer
Give it to me, please.	**Dê-mo, por favor.**	day moo poor fer**voar**
Please bring me...	**Por favor, traga-me...**	poor fer**voar** **trah**ger mer
Bring it to me, please.	**Traga-mo, por favor.**	**trah**ger moo poor fer**voar**
I'm hungry.	**Tenho fome.**	**teh**nyoo **fo**mmer
I'm thirsty.	**Tenho sede.**	**teh**nyoo **say**dher
I'm tired.	**Estou cansada.**	ish**toa** kahng**sah**dher
I'm lost.	**Estou perdido.**	ish**toa** perr**dee**dhoo
It's important.	**É importante.**	eh eeng poor**tahng**ter
It's urgent.	**É urgente.**	eh oor**zhayng**ter
Hurry up!	**Depressa!**	der**preh**sser

*In Brazil: **Entendo/Não entendo** (ayng**tayng**doa/nahng^w ayng**tayng**doa).

SOME BASIC EXPRESSIONS

It is/There is...

It's...	**É...**	eh
Is it...?	**É...?**	eh
There is/There are...	**Há...**	ah
Is there/Are there...?	**Há...?**	ah
There isn't/There aren't...	**Não há...**	nahng^w ah
There isn't any/There aren't any.	**Não há nenhum/Não há nenhuns (Não há nenhuma/Não há nenhumas).**	nahng^w ah nernyoong/ nahng^w ah nernyoongsh (nahng^w ah nernyoomer/ nahng^w ah nernyoomersh)

A few common words

big/small	**grande/pequeno**	grahngder/perkaynoo
quick/slow	**rápido/lento**	rahpidhoo/layngtoo
early/late	**cedo/tarde**	saydhoo/tahrder
cheap/expensive	**barato/caro**	berrahtoo/kahroo
near/far	**perto/longe**	pehrtoo/lawngzher
hot/cold	**quente/frio**	kayngter/freeoo
full/empty	**cheio/vazio**	shayoo/verzeeoo
easy/difficult	**fácil/difícil**	fahssil/diffeessil
heavy/light	**pesado/leve**	perzahdhoo/lehver
open/shut	**aberto/fechado**	erbehrtoo/fershahdhoo
right/wrong	**certo/errado**	sehrtoo/errahdhoo
old/new	**velho/novo**	vehlyoo/noavoo
old/young	**idoso/jovem**	idhoazoo/zhovvayng
beautiful/ugly	**belo/feio**	behloo/fayoo
good/bad	**bom/mau**	bawng/mow
better/worse	**melhor/pior**	merlyor/peeor

Some prepositions and a few more useful words

at	**a**	er
on	**sobre**	soabrer
in	**em**	ayng
to	**para**	perrer
from	**de**	der
inside	**dentro**	dayngtroo
outside	**fora**	forrer
up	**em cima**	ayng seemer
down	**em baixo**	ayng bighshoo
before	**antes**	ahngtersh
after	**depois**	derpawngʸsh
with	**com**	kawng
without	**sem**	sayng
through	**através**	ertrervehsh
towards	**para**	perrer
until	**até**	erteh
during	**durante**	doorahngter
and	**e**	ee
or	**ou**	oa
not	**não**	nahngʷ
nothing	**nada**	nahdher
none	**nenhum**	nernyoong
very	**muito**	moongʸtoo
also	**também**	tahngbayng
soon	**em breve**	ayng brehver
perhaps	**talvez**	tahlvaysh
here	**aqui**	erkee
there	**ali**	erlee
now	**agora**	ergorrer
then	**depois**	derpawngʸsh

Arrival

You've arrived. Whether you've come by ship or plane, you'll have to go through passport and customs formalities. (For car/border control, see page 146).

There's certain to be somebody around who speaks English. That's why we're making this a brief section. What you really want is to be off to your hotel in the shortest possible time. And here are the steps to get these formalities out of the way quickly.

Passport control

Here's my passport.	**Eis aqui o meu passaporte.**	aysh er**kee** oo me**hoo** pahsser**porter**
I'll be staying...	**Fico...**	**fee**koo
a few days	**alguns dias**	ahl**goongsh dee**ersh
a week	**uma semana**	**oo**mer ser**mah**ner
two weeks	**quinze dias**	**keeng**zer **dee**ersh
a month	**um mês**	oong maysh
I don't know yet.	**Ainda não sei.**	er**eeng**dher nahng^w say
I'm here on holiday.	**Estou aqui de férias.**	ish**toa** er**kee** der **feh**ryersh
I'm here on business.	**Estou aqui em [à] negócio.**	ish**toa** er**kee** ayng [ah] ner**goss**yoosh
I'm just passing through.	**Estou de passagem.**	ish**toa** der per**ssah**zhayng

If things become difficult:

I'm sorry, I don't understand.	**Desculpe, não compreendo.**	dersh**kool**per nahng^w kawngprer**ayng**doo
Is there anyone here who speaks English?	**Há aqui alguém que fale inglês?**	ah er**kee** ahl**gayng** ker **fah**ler eeng**glaysh**

Customs

Believe it or not, the customs officials are just as eager to wave you through as you are to go.

The chart below shows what you can bring in duty free.*

	Cigarettes		Cigars		Tobacco (grams)	Spirits (liquor)		Wine
Portugal	200	or	50	or	250	1	and	2
Brazil	400		and		250	1	and	1

In addition to personal clothing, jewellery and a small quantity of perfume, you are also allowed to take in a camera with two rolls of film, a cine (movie) camera with two rolls of film, a pair of binoculars, a portable radio and other items of a personal nature.

Upon arrival, you'll have to collect your luggage before heading for the customs officer. A few spot-checks are made, but otherwise baggage isn't even opened.

I've nothing to declare.	Não tenho nada a declarar.	nahng^w tehnyoo nahdher er derklerrahr
I've a...	Tenho...	tehnyoo
carton of cigarettes	um pacote de cigarros	oong perkotter der siggahrroosh
bottle of whisky/wine	uma garrafa de whisky/vinho	oomer gerrrahfer der weeshkee/veenyoo
Must I pay on this?	Devo pagar por isto?	dayvoo pergahr poor ishtoo
How much?	Quanto?	kwahngtoo
It's for my personal use.	É para uso pessoal.	eh perrer oozoo persswahl
It's not new.	Não é novo.	nahng^w eh noavoo

* All allowances subject to change without notice.

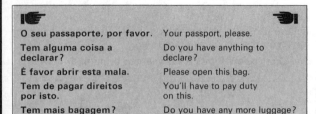

O seu passaporte, por favor.	Your passport, please.
Tem alguma coisa a declarar?	Do you have anything to declare?
É favor abrir esta mala.	Please open this bag.
Tem de pagar direitos por isto.	You'll have to pay duty on this.
Tem mais bagagem?	Do you have any more luggage?

Baggage—Porters

Where no porters are available you'll find luggage trolleys for the use of the passengers.

Porter!	**Bagageiro [Carregador]!**	berger**zhay**roo [kahrraygahd**hoar**]
Please take these bags.	**Leve-me a bagagem, por favor.**	**leh**ver mer er ber**gah**zhayng poor fer**voar**
That's mine.	**Isto é meu.**	**ish**too eh **meh**oo
That's my suitcase.	**Aquela é a minha mala.**	er**keh**ler eh er **mee**nyer **mah**ler
That ... one.	**Aquela...**	er**keh**ler
big/small	**grande/pequena**	**grahng**dher/per**kay**ner
blue/brown	**azul/castanha**	ah**zool**/kersh**tah**nyer
black/plaid	**preta/escocesa**	**pray**ter/ishkoo**ssay**zer
There's one piece missing.	**Falta um volume.**	**fahl**ter oong voo**loo**mer
Take these bags to the...	**Leve-me a bagagem ao...**	**leh**ver mer er ber**gah**zhayng ow
bus	**autocarro [ônibus]**	owtok**kah**rroo [oanib**hooss**]
luggage lockers	**depósito da bagagem**	derpoz**zit**too der ber**gah**zhayng
taxi	**táxi**	**tahk**see
How much is that?	**Quanto é?**	**kwahng**too eh

FOR TIPPING, see page 1

Changing money

You'll find a bank or currency exchange (*agencia de câmbio*—erzhayngsyer der **kahng**byoo) at most airports. If it's closed, don't worry. You'll be able to change money at your hotel. Full details about money and currency exchange are given on pages 134—136.

Where's the nearest currency exchange?	**Onde é agencia de câmbio [o câmbio] mais próximo?**	awngder eh erzhayngsyer der **kahng**byoo [oo **kahng**byoa] mighsh **prossimmoo**
Can you change these traveller's cheques (checks)?	**Pode trocar-me estes cheques de viagem?**	podher trookahr mer ayshtersh **shehk**ersh der vyahzhayng
I want to change some…	**Quero trocar…**	kehroo troo**kahr**
dollars	**dólares**	dollahrersh
pounds	**libras**	leebrersh
Can you change this into escudos/cruzeiros?	**Pode trocar-me isto em escudos/cruzeiros?**	podher trookahr mer **ish**too ayng ish**koodhoosh**/kroozayroass
What's the exchange rate?	**A como está [qual é] o câmbio?**	ah koamoo ishtah [kwahl eh] oo **kahng**byoo

Directions

How do I get to…?	**Como posso ir para…?**	koamoo possoo eer perrer
Where's the bus into town?	**Onde apanho o autocarro [ônibus] para o centro?**	awngder erpernyoo oo owtokkahrroo [oanibhooss] perrer oo **sayng**troo
Where can I get a taxi?	**Onde apanho [pego] um táxi?**	awngder erpernyoo [pehgoo] oong **tahk**see
Where can I rent a car?	**Onde posso alugar um carro?**	awngder possoo erloo**gahr** oong **kahr**roo

FOR NUMBERS, see page 175

Car rental

There are car rental firms at most airports and terminals. It's highly likely that someone there speaks English. But if nobody does, try one of the following:

I'd like a...	**Queria alugar um...**	kerreeer erloogahr oong
car	**carro**	kahrroo
small car	**carro pequeno**	kahrroo perkehnoo
large car	**carro grande**	kahrroo grahngdher
sports car	**carro «sport» [esporte]**	kahrroo sport [isportee]
I'd like it for...	**Queria-o por...**	kerreeer oo poor
a day/4 days	**um dia/4 dias**	oong deeer/4 deeersh
a week/2 weeks	**uma semana/2 semanas**	oomer sermahner/ 2 sermahnersh
What's the charge per...	**Qual é a tarifa por...**	kwahl eh er terreefer poor
day/week	**dia/semana**	deeer/sermahner
Does that include mileage?	**A quilometragem está incluída?**	er killommertrahzhayng ishtah eengklweedher
What's the charge per kilometre?	**Quanto custa o quilómetro?**	kwahngtoo kooshter oo killommertroo
Is petrol (gasoline) included?	**Está incluído o preço da gasolina?**	ishtah eengklweedhoo oo prayssoo der gerzooleener
I want full insurance.	**Quero seguro contra todos os riscos.**	kehroo sergooroo kawngtrer toadhoosh oosh reeshkoosh
What's the deposit?	**De quanto é o depósito?**	der kwahngtoo eh oo derpozzittoo
I've a credit card.	**Tenho uma carta de crédito.**	tehnyoo oomer kahrter der krehdhittoo
Here's my driving licence.	**Aqui está a minha carta de condução [carteira de motorista].**	erkee ishtah er meenyer kahrter der kawngdhoossahng^w [kahrtayrah di moatoareeestah]

You must be at least 21 (25 for some firms) years old to hire a car, and have a valid driving licence held for at least one year.

FOR SIGHTSEEING, see page 75

Taxi

Not all Portuguese taxis have meters, so it's best to ask the approximate fare beforehand. There is a night surcharge.

In Brazil, fare increases occur so often that it is impractical to keep readjusting the meters. A table of equivalents tells the driver what to charge you.

Where can I get a taxi?	**Onde posso encontrar um táxi?**	awngder possoo ayngkawngtrahr oong tahksee
Please get me a taxi.	**Chame-me um táxi, por favor.**	shahmer mer oong tahksee poor fervoar
What's the fare to...?	**Qual é o preço do percurso [da corrida] para...?**	kwahl eh oo prayssoo doo perrkoorsoo [dah koarreedhah] perrer
How far is it to...?	**A que distância fica...?**	er ker distahngsyer feeker
Take me to...	**Leve-me...**	lehver mer
this adress	**a esta morada [este endereço]**	ah ehshter moorahdher [aysti ayngdayrayssoa]
to the town centre	**ao centro da cidade**	ow sayngtroo der sidhahdher
the...Hotel	**ao Hotel...**	ow ottehl
Turn...at the next corner.	**Vire...na próxima esquina.**	veerer...ner prossimmer ishkeener
left/right	**à esquerda/à direita**	ah ishkayrdher/ah dirrayter
Go straight ahead.	**Vá sempre em frente.**	vah sayngprer ayng frayngter
Please stop here.	**Páre aqui, por favor.**	pahrer erkee poor fervoar
I'm in a hurry.	**Estou com pressa.**	ishtoa koong prehsser
Could you drive more slowly?	**Pode ir mais devagar?**	podher eer mighsh dervahgahr
Could you help me carry my bags?	**Pode levar-me a bagagem?**	podher lervahr mer er bergahzhayng
How much is it?	**Quanto é?**	kwahngtoo eh

ARRIVAL

FOR TIPPING, see page 1

Hotel – Other accommodation

Early reservation and confirmation are essential in major tourist centres during the high season. But if you're stuck without a room, go to the tourist information office (*turismo*—too**reesh**moo). You'll find one in most towns.

Hotel
(o**ttehl**)

There are seven official categories for hotels in Portugal: international-luxury class A and B, luxury class, first class A, first class B, second and third class; you may still find price variations within the same category, depending on the location and the facilities offered.

Pousada
(poa**zah**dher)

A state-owned inn (Portugal) in the regional style, built near main roads or historical sites. It's cheap, comfortable and serves good food. You're allowed to stay for only 5 days during high season.

Estalagem
(ershter**lah**zhayng)

Similar to the pousada, but more expensive; a privately owned inn.

Motel
(mo**ttehl**)

Increasingly expanding, especially in Brazil; motels offer *dormida e pequeno almoço* (Portugal) or *pernoite e café da manhã* (Brazil)—bed and breakfast.

Pensão
(payng**sahng**ʷ)

Corresponds to a boarding house. Usually divided into three categories: luxury, first class and second class. It offers *pensão completa* (full board) or *dormida e pequeno almoço[pernoite e café da manhã]* (bed and breakfast).

Albergue da juventude
(ahl**behr**ger der zhoovayng**too**dher)

Youth hostel (Portugal). You'll find Y.M.C.A. accommodation in Lisbon, and a few youth hostels on the coast.

Note: Furnished flats (apartments) or bungalows are available through specialized real estate agents.

In this section, we're mainly concerned with the smaller and medium-priced hotels and boarding houses. You'll have no language difficulties in the luxury and first class hotels where most of the staff speak English.

In the next few pages we consider your requirements—step by step—from arrival to departure. You needn't read through all of it; just turn to the situation that applies.

Checking in—Reception

My name is...	O meu nome é...	oo mehoo nommer eh
I've a reservation.	Tenho uma reserva feita.	tehnyoo oomer rerzehrver fayter
We've reserved two rooms, a single and a double.	Reservámos dois quartos, um indivi-dual [de solteiro] e um de casal.	rerzervahmoosh doysh kwahrtoosh oong eengdiv-vidwahl [di soltayroa] ee oong dee kerzahl
I wrote to you last month.	Escrevi-lhe o mês passado.	ishkrervee lyer oo maysh perssahdhoo
Here's the confir-mation.	Aqui está a confirmação.	erkee ishtah er kawngfeermerssahng*
I'd like a...	Queria um...	kerreeer oong
single room	quarto individual	kwahrtoo eengdivvidwahl
double room	quarto de casal	kwahrtoo der kerzahl
I'd like a room...	Queria um quarto...	kerreeer oong kwahrtoo
with twin beds	com duas camas	kawng dooersh kahmersh
with a bath	com casa de banho	kawng kazer der bahnyoo
with a shower	com chuveiro	kawng shoovayroo
with a balcony	com varanda	kawng verrahngder
with a view	com vista	kawng veeshter
We'd like a room...	Queríamos um quarto...	kerreeermoosh oong kwahrtoo
in the front	na frente	ner frayngter
at the back	nas traseiras [de fundos]	nersh trerzayrersh [di foondoss]
facing the sea	com vista para o mar	kawng veeshter perrer oo mahr
facing the courtyard	dando para o pátio	dahngdoo perrer oo pahtyoo

It must be quiet.	Deve ser tranquilo.	dehver sayr trahngkweeloo
Is there...?	Há...?	ah
air conditioning	ar condicionado	ahr kawngdhissyoonahdhoo
heating	aquecimento	erkehssimayngtoo
a radio/television in the room	rádio/televisão no quarto	rahdhyoo/terlervizzahng^w noo kwahrtoo
a laundry service	serviço de lavandaria	sehrveessoo der lahvahngderreeer
room service	serviço de quartos	sehrveessoo dee kwahrtoosh
hot water	água quente	ahgwer kayngter
running water	água corrente	ahgwer koorayngter
a private toilet	casa de banho [privada] particular	kazer der bahnyoo [privvahdhah] perrtikkoolahr

How much?

What's the price...?	Qual é o preço...?	kwahl eh oo prayssoo
per week/night	por semana/noite	poor sermahner/nawng^yter
for bed and breakfast	por dormida e pequeno almoço*	poor doormeedher ee perkaynoo ahlmoassoo
excluding meals	sem refeições	sayng rerfayssawng^ysh
for full board	por [da] pensão completa	poor [dah] payngsahng^w kawngplehter
Does that include...?	O preço inclui...?	oo prayssoo eengklooi
breakfast	pequeno almoço [café da manhã]	perkaynoo ahlmoassoo [kahfeh dah mahnyahng]
meals	refeições	rerfayssawng^ysh
service	serviço	sehrveessoo
tax	imposto	eengpoashtoo
Is there any reduction for children?	Fazem redução às crianças?	fahzayng rerdhoossahng^w ersh kryahngssersh
Do you charge for the baby?	O bébé paga?	oo behbheh pahger
That's too expensive.	É caro demais.	eh kahroo dermighsh
Haven't you anything cheaper?	Não há nada mais barato?	nahng^w ah nahdher mighsh berrahtoo

* In Brazil: **pernoite e café da manhã** (pehr**nawng**^yter ee kah**feh** dah mahng**nyahng**).

FOR NUMBERS, see page 175

How long?

We'll be staying…	**Ficamos…**	fikkermoosh
overnight only	**só uma noite**	so oomer nawng^{y}ter
a few days	**alguns dias**	ahlgoongsh deeersh
a week (at least)	**uma semana (pelo menos)**	oomer sermahner (perloo maynoosh)
I don't know yet.	**Ainda não sei.**	ereengder nahng^w say

Decision

May I see the room?	**Posso ver o quarto?**	possoo vayr oo kwahrtoo
No, I don't like it.	**Não, não gosto.**	nahng^w nahng^w goshtoo
It's too…	**É muito…**	eh moong^{y}too
cold/hot	**frio/quente**	freeoo/kayngter
dark/small	**escuro/pequeno**	ishkooroo/perkaynoo
noisy	**barulhento**	berroolyayngtoo
I asked for a room with a bath.	**Pedi um quarto com banho.**	perdhee oong kwahrtoo kawng bernyoo
Do you have anything…?	**Tem alguma coisa…**	tayng ahlgoomer kawng^{v}zer
better/bigger	**melhor/maior**	merlyor/mighor
cheaper/quieter	**mais barata/mais tranquila**	mighsh berrahter/mighsh trahngkweeler
higher up/lower down	**mais alto/num andar inferior**	mighsh ahltoo/noong ahngdahr eengferryoar
Do you have a room with a better view?	**Tem um quarto com melhor vista?**	tayng oong kwahrtoo kawng merlyor veeshter
That's fine. I'll take it.	**Está bem. Fico com ele.**	ishtah bayng. feekoo kawng ayler

HOTEL

Bills

These are usually paid weekly or upon departure if you stay less than a week. Most hotels offer a reduction of 35 per cent for children under 8 when sleeping in the parents' room. In Brazil, the reduction for children can vary from 35 to 50 per cent.

Tipping

A service charge is normally included in the bill in Portugal, but you can ask:

Is service included?	**Está incluído o serviço?**	ishtah eengklweedhoo oo serrveessoo

In Brazil, some hotels include service, others don't. Check the notices.

Registration

Upon arrival at a hotel or boarding house you'll be asked to fill in a registration form (*uma ficha*—**oo**mer **fee**sher). It asks your name, home address, passport number and further destination. It's almost certain to carry an English translation. If it doesn't, ask the desk-clerk (*porteiro*—poor**tay**roo).

What does this mean?	**Que significa isto?**	ker signiffeeker ishtoo

The desk-clerk will probably ask you for your passport. He may want to keep it for a while, even overnight. Don't worry. You'll get it back. He may want to ask you the following questions:

Posso ver o seu passaporte?	May I see your passport?
Queira preencher esta ficha, faz favor.	Would you mind filling in this registration form?
Assine aqui, por favor.	Please sign here.
Quanto tempo vai ficar?	How long will you be staying?

What's my room number?	**Qual é o número do meu quarto?**	kwahl eh oo noomerroo doo mehoo kwahrtoo
Will you have our bags sent up?	**Pode mandar subir as nossas malas?**	podher mahngdahr soobheer ersh nossersh mahlersh

FOR TIPPING, see page 1

HOTEL

Service, please

bellboy	**paquete/groom** [mensageiro]	perkayter/groom [mayngsahzhayroa]
maid	**a criada de quarto** [a arrumadeira]	er kryahdher der kwahrtoo [ah ahrroomahdayrah]
manager	**o gerente**	oo zherrayngter
switchboard operator	**a telefonista**	er terlerfooneeshter
waiter	**o criado de mesa** [o garçom]	oo kryahdhoo der mayzer [oo gahrsawng]
waitress	**a criada de mesa** [a garçonete]	er kryahdher der mayzer [ah gahrsonnehti]

Call the members of the staff *senhor* (ser**nyoar**), *senhora* (ser-**nyo**rrer) or *senhorita* (sernyoa**ree**ter).

General requirements

Please ask the maid to come up.	**Por favor, chame a criada de quarto** [arrumadeira].	poor fervoar shahmer er kryahdher der kwahrtoo [ahrroomahdayrah]
Who is it?	**Quem é?**	kayng eh
Just a minute.	**Um momento.**	oong moomayngtoo
Come in.	**Entre.**	ayngtrer
Is there a bath on this floor?	**Há uma casa de banho** [um banheiro] **neste andar?**	ah oomer kahzer der bahnyoo [oong bahnyay-roa] nayshter ahngdahr
Where's the plug for the razor?	**Onde está a tomada para a máquina de barbear** [barbeador elétrico]?	awngder ishtah er toomah-dher perrer er mahkinner der berrberahr [bahrbyah-dhoar illehtrikkoa]
What's the voltage here?	**Qual é a voltagem aqui?**	kwahl eh er voltahzhayng erkee
Can we have breakfast in our room?	**Podemos tomar o pequeno almoço** [café da manhã] **no quarto?**	poodhaymoosh toomahr oo perkaynoo ahlmoassoo [kahfeh dah mahnyahng] noo kwahrtoo
I'd like to leave this in your safe.	**Gostaria de deixar isto no cofre do hotel.**	gooshterreeer der dayshahr ishtoo noo kofrer doo ottehl

May I have a/an/some...?	Pode dar-me...?	podher dahr mer
ashtray	um cinzeiro	oong seengzayroo
bath towel	uma toalha de banho	oomer twahlyer der bahnyoo
extra blanket	mais um cobertor	mighsh oong kooberrtoar
envelopes	envelopes	ayngverloppersh
(more) hangers	(mais) alguns cabides	(mighsh) ahlgoongsh kerbheedhersh
ice cubes	cubos de gelo	koobhoosh der zhayloo
extra pillow	mais uma almofada [um travesseiro]	mighsh oomer ahlmoo-fahdher [oong trah-vayssayroa]
reading lamp	um candeeiro [abajur]	oong kahngdyayroo [ahbhahzhoor]
soap	sabão	serbahng\u02b7
writing paper	papel de carta	perpehl der kahrter
Where's the...?	Onde é...?	awngder eh
barber's	o barbeiro	oo berrbayroo
bathroom	a casa de banho [o banheiro]	er kahzer der bahnyoo [oo bahnyayroa]
beauty parlour	o salão de beleza	oo serlahng\u02b7 der berlayzer
dining-room	a sala de jantar	er sahler der zhahngtahr
hairdresser's	o cabeleireiro	oo kerberlayrayroo
restaurant	o restaurante	oo rershtowrahngter
television room	a sala de televisão	er sahler der terlervi-zzahng\u02b7
toilet	a retrete [a privada]	er rertrehter [ah privvahdhah]

Breakfast

The Portuguese breakfast consists of coffee (black or with milk), rolls, butter and jam, seldom marmalade. Most of the larger hotels, however, are now used to providing an English or American breakfast.

I'll have a/an/some...	Traga-me...	trahger mer
bacon and eggs	ovos com toucinho	ovvoosh kawng toa-sseenyoo
cereals	cornflakes	"cornflakes"
eggs	ovos	ovvoosh
boiled egg	ovo cozido	oavoo koozeedhoo
soft/medium/hard	quente/médio/duro	kayngter/mehdhyoo/dooroo

fried eggs	**ovos estrelados**	ovvoosh ishtrerlahdhoosh
scrambled eggs	**ovos mexidos**	ovvoosh mersheedhoosh
fruit juice	**sumo [suco] de fruta**	soomoo [sookoo] der frooter
grapefruit	**toranja [grapefruit]**	toorahngzher [graypifrootil]
orange	**laranja**	lerrahngzher
ham and eggs	**ovos com presunto**	ovvoosh kawng prerzoongtoo
jam	**compota [geléia]**	kawngpotter [zhaylehyah]
marmalade	**doce [geléia] de laranja**	doasser [zhaylehyah] der lerrahngzher
toast	**torradas**	toorrahdhersh
May I have some...?	**Pode dar-me...?**	podher dahr mer
hot/cold milk	**leite quente/frio**	layter kayngter/freeoo
cream/sugar	**nata [creme]/açúcar**	nahter [kraymi]/erssookahr
bread/rolls	**pão/pãezinhos**	pahngʷ/pahngʸzeenyoosh
butter	**manteiga**	mahngtayger
salt/pepper	**sal/pimenta**	sahl/pimmayngter
coffee/tea	**café/chá**	kerfeh/shah
hot chocolate	**chocolate quente**	shookoolahter kayngter
lemon/honey	**limão/mel**	limmahngʷ/mehl
hot water	**água quente**	ahgwer kayngter
Could you bring me a...?	**Pode trazer-me...?**	podher trerzayr mer
plate	**um prato**	oong prahtoo
glass	**um copo**	oong koppoo
cup	**uma chávena [xícara]**	oomer shahverner [sheekahrah]
knife/fork	**uma faca/um garfo**	oomer fahker/oong gahrfoo
napkin	**um guardanapo**	oong gwerrdernahpoo
spoon	**uma colher**	oomer koolyehr

Difficulties

The...doesn't work.	**...não funciona.**	nahngʷ foongsionner
air-conditioner	**o ar condicionado**	oo ahr kawngdhissyoonahdhoo
fan	**a ventoinha [o ventilador]**	er vayngtweenyer/[oo vayngtillerdhoar]
heating	**o aquecimento**	oo erkehssimmayngtoo
light	**a luz**	er loozh
radio	**o rádio**	oo rahdhyoo

FOR EATING OUT, see pages 38–64

tap	a torneira	er toornayrer
toilet	a retrete	er rertrehter
	[a privada]	[ah privvahdah]
ventilator	a ventilação	er vayngtillerssahng^w
The wash-basin is clogged.	O lavatório está entupido [A pia está entupida].	oo lervertorryoo ishtah ayngtoopeedhoo [ah peeah istah ayngtoopeedhah]
The window is jammed.	A janela está empenada [com defeito].	er zhernehler ishtah ayngpernahdher [kawng dayfaytoa]
The door won't lock.	A porta não fecha.	er porter nahng^w fehsher
There's no hot water.	Não há água quente.	nahng^w ah ahgwer kayngter
I've left my key in my room.	Deixei a chave no quarto.	dayshay er shahver noo kwahrtoo
The bulb is burnt out.	A lâmpada fundiu-se [queimou].	er lahngperdher foongdioo ser [kaymoa]
The...is broken.	...está partido/a [quebrado/a].	...ishtah perrteedhoo/er [kaybrahdhoa/ah]
lamp	o candeeiro [abajur]	oo kahngdyayroo [ahbahzhoor]
plug	a tomada	er toomahdher
shutter	a persiana [veneziana]	er perrsyahner [vaynayzyahnah]
switch	o interruptor	oo eengterrootoar
venetian blind	a gelosia	er zherloozeeer
window shade	o toldo	oo toaldoo
Can you get it repaired?	Pode repará-lo [consertá-lo]?	podher rerperrah loo [kawngsehrtah loa]

Telephone—Mail—Callers

Can you get me Lisbon 123456?	Pode ligar-me para o 123456 em Lisboa?	podher liggahr mer perrer oo 123456 ayng lizhboaer
Did anyone telephone me?	Alguém me telefonou?	ahlgayng mer terlerfoonoa
Do you have stamps?	Tem selos?	tayng sayloosh
Would you please mail this for me?	Pode pôr-me isto no correio, por favor?	podher poar mer ishtoo noo koorrayoo poor fervoar

FOR POST OFFICE and TELEPHONE, see pages 137–138

Checking out

		er toornayrer
		er rertrehter
May I please have my bill?	**Pode dar-me a conta, por favor?**	podher dahr mer er kawngter poor fervoar
I'm leaving early tomorrow. Please have my bill ready.	**Parto amanhã cedo. Prepare a minha conta, por favor.**	pahrtoo ahmernyahng saydhoo. prerpahrer er meenyer kawngter poor fervoar
We'll be checking out around noon.	**Partimos por volta do meio-dia**	perrteemoosh poor volter doo mayoo deeer
I must leave at once.	**Tenho de partir imediatamente.**	tehnyoo der perrteer immerdhyahtermayngter
Is everything included?	**Está tudo incluído?**	ishtah toodhoo eeng-klweedhoo
You've made a mistake in this bill, I think.	**Penso que se enganou na conta.**	payngsoo ker ser aynggernoa ner kawngter
Can you get us a taxi?	**Pode chamar-nos um táxi?**	podher shermahr noosh oong tahksi
When's the next... to Sintra?	**A que horas parte o próximo...para Sintra?**	er ker orrersh pahrter oo prossimmoo... perrer seengtrer
bus	**autocarro [ônibus]**	owtookkahrroo [oanibhooss]
train	**comboio [trem]**	kawngboyoo [trayng]
plane	**avião**	ervyahng^w
Would you send someone to bring down our baggage?	**Pode mandar descer a nossa bagagem?**	podher mahngdahr derssayr er nosser bergahzhayng
We're in a great hurry.	**Temos muita pressa.**	tehmoosh moong^yter prehsser
Here's the forwarding address.	**Eis o meu próximo endereço.**	aysh oo mehoo prossimmoo ayngderrayssoo
You have my home address.	**Já tem o meu endereço particular.**	zhah tayng oo mehoo ayngderrayssoo perrtikkoolahr
It's been a very enjoyable stay.	**Tivemos uma óptima estadia.**	tivvehmoosh oomer ottimmer ishterdheeer
I hope we'll come again sometime.	**Esperamos voltar.**	ishperrahmoosh voaltahr

HOTEL SERVICE

FOR TAXI, see page 27

Eating out

From snack bars to luxury restaurants, eating out can be one of the most interesting experiences of your trip. Here are some of the types of eating and drinking places you'll come across. In Portugal the most distinctive are the *pousadas* and the *casas de fado* or *adegas típicas*, the little restaurants where you eat or drink to the sound of the *fado*, the national folk song.

In Brazil, don't miss the *churrascarias*, restaurants specializing in excellent barbecues.

Café-Bar (kerfeh bahr)	Coffee shop and bar, where hot and cold drinks are served; you'll often be able to get a snack there.
Casa de fado (kahzer der fahdhoo)	A typical Portuguese restaurant, where you can listen to the famous *fado* songs, accompanied by guitars; the best known are located in the old districts of Lisbon (*Bairro de Alfama, Bairro Alto*).
Churrasqueira (shoorrershkayrer)	Restaurant; specializes in chicken.
Churrascarias (shoorrahskahreeahss)	Restaurant; specializing in barbecue, a *churrascaria* offers a great variety of grilled meat, generally served with fried potatoes and a hot sauce of onions, tomatoes and green peppers (Brazil).
Confeitaria (kawngfayterreeer)	A cake shop, also serving coffee, tea and other drinks.
Estalagem (ishterlahzhayng)	Privately-owned inn, serving regional specialities.
Pastelaria (pershterlerreeer)	The same as a *confeitaria*.
Pousada (poazahdher)	State inn, specializing in local dishes; often located near highways or places of interest for tourists.

Restaurante (rershtow**rahng**ter)	According to the cuisine and service's standard: *de luxo* (luxury), *de primeira, de segunda* or *de terceira classe* (first, second or third class).
Salão de chá (ser**lahng**ʷ der shah)	A smart tea-shop.
Snack-Bar (snahk bahr)	The same as at home.

Meal times

In this section, we're primarily concerned with lunch and dinner. We assume that you've had breakfast at your hotel —see page 34 for a breakfast menu. Lunch (*o almoço*—oo ahl**moa**ssoo) is generally served from 1 p.m. to 3 p.m. in both Portugal and Brazil.

Dinner (*o jantar*—oo zhahng**tahr**) is served far later than at home in a Portuguese *casa de fado* (around 9 p.m.), where the show is likely to start around 10 p.m. In ordinary restaurants, though, *jantar* is served from 7.30 p.m. to 9 p.m.

Brazilians are used to eating late in the evening (dinner time is 8 p.m. to 11 p.m.); they like to linger over a meal, so don't be surprised if service is slow: you're expected to take your time.

Eating habits

Most Portuguese and Brazilian restaurants display a menu (*ementa* in Portugal, *cardápio* in Brazil) outside. Besides the à la carte items, it may offer one or more set menus. The service charge (*serviço,* in Brazil sometimes called *couvert*) of 10 per cent is often, but not always included. A tip is up to you; for a snack some small change will do, and if you've had a really good meal you might like to leave an extra 5 per cent on the table for the waiter.

On some set menus you'll notice that wine is included *(vinho incluído)*.

A *prato do dia* (**prah**too doo **dee**er—day's special) usually offers you a good meal at a fair price. A word like *especiali-dade* next to a dish listed on the menu is a clue that the dish is a speciality of the restaurant.

O que deseja?	What would you like?
Aconselho isto	I recommend this.
O que deseja beber?	What would you like to drink?
Não temos...	We haven't got...
Deseja...?	Do you want...?

Hungry

I'm hungry/I'm thirsty.	**Tenho fome/ Tenho sede.**	tehnyoo fommer/ tehnyoo saydher
Can you recommend a good restaurant?	**Pode aconselhar- -me um bom restaurante?**	podher erkawngserlyahr mer oong bawng rersh- towrahngter
Are there any good, cheap restaurants around here?	**Há um bom restau- rante barato aqui perto?**	ah oong bawng rershtow- rahngter berrahtoo erkee pehrtoo

If you want to be sure of getting a table in a well-known restaurant or a *casa de fado*, it may be better to telephone in advance.

I'd like to reserve a table for 4.	**Queria reservar uma mesa para 4 pessoas.**	kerreeer rerzerrvahr oomer mayzer perrer 4 perssoaersh
We'll come at 8.	**Chegamos [Viremos] às 8.**	shergahmoosh [virray- moass] ahsh 8

Asking and ordering

Good evening. I'd like a table for 3.	**Boa noite. Queria uma mesa para 3 pessoas.**	boaer nawng^vter. kerreeer oomer mayzer perrer 3 perssoaersh
Could we have a table...?	**Podemos ter uma mesa...?**	poodhehmoosh tayr oomer mayzer
in the corner	**ao [no] canto**	ow [noa] kahngtoo
by the window	**perto da janela**	pehrtoo der zhernehler
outside	**ao ar livre/fora**	ow ahr leevrer/forrer
on the terrace	**no terraço**	noo terrahssoo
May I please have the menu?	**Pode dar-me a ementa [o cardápio]?**	podher dahr mer er immayngter [oa kahr-dahpyoa]
What's this?	**O que é isto?**	oo ker eh ishtoo
Do you have...?	**Tem...?**	tayng
a set menu	**uma ementa fixa [um menu feito]**	oomer immayngter feekser [oong mehnoo faytoa]
local dishes	**pratos típicos**	prahtoosh teepikkoosh
a children's menu	**uma ementa [pratos] para crianças**	oomer immayngter [prahtoass] perrer kryahngsersh
I'd like...	**Queria...**	kerreeer
Is service included?	**o serviço [couvert] está incluído?**	oo serrveessoo [koovehr] ishtah eengklweedhoo
Could we have a/an ...please?	**Pode dar-nos... por favor?**	podher dahr noosh... poor fervoar
ashtray	**um cinzeiro**	oong seengzayroo
another chair	**outra cadeira**	oatrer kerdhayrer
fork	**um garfo**	oong gahrfoo
glass	**um copo**	oong koppoo
knife	**uma faca**	oomer fahker
napkin (serviette)	**um guardanapo**	oong gwerrdernahpoo
plate	**um prato**	oong prahtoo
spoon	**uma colher**	oomer koolyehr
I'd like a/an/some...	**Queria...**	kerreeer
aperitif	**um aperitivo**	oong erperritteevoo
appetizers	**uns acepipes [uns salgadinhos]**	oongsh ersserpeepersh [oongs sahlgahdhee-nyoass]
beer	**uma cerveja**	oomer serrvayzher

EATING OUT

FOR COMPLAINTS, see page 57

bread	**pão**	pahng^w
butter	**manteiga**	mahngtayger
cabbage	**couve-lombarda** [couve]	koaver lawngbahrdher [koavi]
chips	**batatas fritas**	bertahtersh freetersh
cheese	**queijo**	kayzhoo
coffee	**café**	kerfeh
dessert	**uma sobremesa**	oomer soobrermayzer
fish	**peixe**	paysher
french fries	**batatas fritas**	bertahtersh freetersh
fruit	**fruta**	frooter
game	**caça**	kahsser
ice-cream	**um gelado [um sorvete]**	oong zherlahdhoo[oong sorvayti]
ketchup	**molho ketchup**	moalyoo kehtsherp
lemon	**limão**	limmahng^w
lettuce	**alface**	ahlfahsser
meat	**carne**	kahrner
mineral water	**uma água mineral**	oomer ahgwer minnerrahl
milk	**leite**	layter
mustard	**mostarda**	mooshtahrder
noodles	**massa**	mahsser
(olive) oil	**azeite (de oliva)**	erzayter (der olleever)
pepper	**pimenta**	pimmayngter
potatoes	**batatas**	bertahtersh
poultry	**aves**	ahversh
rice	**arroz**	errroash
rolls	**uns pãezinhos**	oongsh pahng^yzeenyoosh
saccharine	**sacarina**	serkerreener
salad	**uma salada**	oomer serlahdher
salt	**sal**	sahl
sandwich	**uma [um] sanduíche**	oomer [oong] sahng-dweesher
seafood	**mariscos**	merreeshkoosh
seasoning	**tempero**	tayngpayroo
soup	**uma sopa**	oomer soaper
starter	**uns acepipes [uns salgadinhos]**	oongsh erserpeepersh [oongs sahlgahdheenyoass]
sugar	**açúcar**	erssookahr
tea	**chá**	shah
vegetables	**legumes**	lergoomersh
(iced) water	**água (com gelo)**	ahgwer (kawng zhayloo)
wine	**vinho**	veenyoo

What's on the menu?

Our menu is presented according to courses. Under the headings below you'll find alphabetical lists of dishes that might be offered on a Portuguese menu with their English equivalent. You can also show the book to the waiter. If you want some fruit, for instance, show him the appropriate list and let *him* point to what's available. Use pages 41 and 42 for ordering in general.

Here then is our guide to good eating and drinking. Turn to the section you want.

	page
Appetizers	44
Salad	45
Soup	46
Egg dishes and omelets	46
Fish and seafood	47
Meat	49
Game and fowl	51
Vegetables	52
Cheese	54
Fruit	55
Dessert	56
Drinks	58
Eating light—Snacks	64

Obviously, you're not going to go through every course. If you've had enough, say:

Nothing more, thanks.	**Mais nada, obrigado.**	mighsh **nah**dher oobri**gga**hdhoo

EATING OUT

Appetizers

I'd like an appetizer.	**Queria uns acepipes [uns salgadinhos].**	kerreeer oongsh ersserpeepersh [oongs sahlgahd**hee**nyoass]
acepipes variados	ersserpeepersh verryah-dhoosh	assorted appetizers
aipo	ighpoo	celery
agulha frita	ergoolyer **free**ter	fried garfish
alcachofras	ahlkershoafrersh	artichokes
ameijoas	ermayzhwersh	clams
anchovas	ahngshoaversh	anchovies
arroz de atum	errroash der ertoong	blended rice and tuna fish
arroz de tomate	errroash der toomahter	rice with tomato and onions
atum	ertoong	tuna
azeitonas (recheadas)	erzaytoanersh (rershyah**dh**ersh)	(stuffed) olives
bolinhos de bacalhau	boaleenyoosh der ber-kerlyow	croquettes of dried cod and potatoes
camarões	kermer**rawng**ʸsh	shrimp
caracóis	kerrerkoysh	snails
caranguejo	kerrahng**gay**zhoo	crab
castanhas de cajú	kersh**tah**nyersh der kah**zh**oo	cashew nuts
cogumelos	koogoomehloosh	mushrooms
enguia	aynggeeer	eel
espargos	ishpahrgoosh	asparagus
favas	fahversh	broad beans
à Algarvia	er ahl**ger**rvyer	with chicken stock, sausage and ham
à saloia	ah serlawngʸer	with chopped bacon and sausage
fiambre	fyahngbrer	gammon (ham)
fígado de ganso	feegerdhoo der **gahng**soo	goose-liver
melão	merlahng**ʷ**	melon
com vinho do Porto	kawng **vee**nyoo doo **poar**too	soaked in Port wine
mexilhões	mershil**lyawng**ʸsh	mussels
ostras	oashtrersh	oysters
do Algarve	doo ahl**gahr**ver	baked in butter and dry wine
recheadas	rershyah**dh**ersh	in a cream sauce with onions
paio	**pigh**oo	cured pork sausage

pimentos	pimmayngtoosh	peppers
presunto	prerzoongtoo	cured ham
cru	kroo	raw ham
com figos	kawng feegoosh	with figs
salgadinhos	sahlgahdheenyoas	assorted appetizers
variados	vahryahdhoas	(Braz.)
sardinhas	serdeenyersh	sardines
sumo [suco] de	soomoo [sookoo] der	fruit juice
fruta	frooter	
laranja	lerrahngzher	orange
tomate	toomahter	tomato
tomates recheados	toomahtersh rershyah-dhoosh	baked tomatoes, stuffed with bread and cheese, or with meat or rice

casquinhas de caranguejo (kahskeenyahss dee kahrahnggayzhoa)	crab shells filled with seasoned crab meat (Braz.)
chouriço (shoareessoo)	smoked pork sausage seasoned with paprika and garlic
empadinhas de atum (ayngperdheenyersh der ertoong)	small tuna pies flavoured with spirits

Eggs

Egg dishes are popular in Portugal, and they're often offered as an alternative to soup or hors-d'œuvre, or as a second course. Portuguese cooks usually prepare them with olive oil or margarine.

ovos	ovvoosh	eggs
cozidos	koozeedhoosh	boiled eggs
duros	dooroosh	hard-boiled eggs
à Minhota	ah minnyotter	baked in casserole, with tomato, onions
omelete	oomerlehter	omelet
de camarões	der kermerrawngᵛsh	shrimp
de chouriço	der shoareessoo	smoked sausage
de cogumelos	der koogoomehloosh	mushroom
de marisco	der merreeshkoo	shellfish
de presunto	der prerzoongtoo	ham

EATING OUT

Soups

I'd like some soup. What do you recommend?	**Queria sopa. O que me aconselha?**	kerreeer **soa**per. oo ker mer erkawng**say**lyer
açorda de alho	erssoarder der **ah**lyoo	bread soup with garlic and herbs
canja	**kahng**zher	chicken broth with rice
sopa	**soa**per	soup
à pescador	er pershker**dhoar**	fish soup
de agriões	der ergrya**wng**ˈsh	watercress soup
de alho	der **ah**lyoo	garlic-flavoured broth
de feijão	der fay**zhahng**ʷ	red beans purée and cabbage
de feijão verde	der fay**zhahng**ʷ **vay**rder	runner beans, potato purée and herbs
de feijão frade	der fay**zhahng**ʷ **frah**dher	black-eyed beans soup
de grão	der **grahng**ʷ	chick-pea soup, onion and spinach
de legumes	der ler**goo**mersh	vegetable soup
de mariscos	der mer**reesh**koosh	shellfish soup
de mexilhão	der mershil**lyahng**ʷ	mussels soup
Transmontana	trahngzhmawng**tah**ner	vegetable and pork soup with slices of bread

gaspacho
(gershpah**shoo**)

a cold soup made of tomatoes, peppers, cucumbers, served with diced bread

caldo verde
(**kahl**doo **vay**rder)

green, finely shredded kale in a clear potato broth with slices of dried smoked sausage (*chouriço*)

sopa de tomate à Portuguesa
(**soa**per der too**mah**ter ah poortoo**gay**zer)

tomato, garlic, onions, with poached eggs and bread

Fish and seafood

While touring in coastal areas, don't miss the opportunity to sample some of the wide variety of fresh fish and seafood.

I'd like some fish.	**Queria peixe.**	kerr**eeer** pay**sher**
What kind of seafood do you have?	**Que espécies [tipos] de marisco tem?**	ker ish**pehss**yersh [**teepoas**] der mer**reesh**koo tayng

ameijoas	er**mayzh**wersh	clams
anchovas	ahng**shoa**versh	anchovies
arenque	er**rayng**ker	herring
atum	er**toong**	tunny (tuna)
bacalhau	berker**lyow**	cod
calamares	kerler**mah**rersh	squid
camarões	kermer**rawng**ᵛsh	shrimp
camarões grandes	kah**mah**rawngᵛss **grahng**diss	scampi (Braz.)
caranguejo	kerrahng**gay**zhoo	crab
carapau	kerrer**pow**	mackerel
cherne	**shehr**ner	grouper
choco	**shoa**koo	cuttlefish
congro	**kawng**groo	conger
enguia	ayng**geeer**	eel
esturjão	ishtoor**zhahng**ᵂ	sturgeon
gambas	**gahng**bersh	scampi
lagostins	lergoosh**teeng**sh	prawns
lampreia	lahng**prayer**	lamprey
linguado	leeng**gwah**dhoo	sole
lula	**loo**ler	squid
mexilhões	mershi**lyawng**ᵛsh	mussels
ostras	**oash**trersh	oysters
pargo	**pahr**goo	sea bream
peixe agulha	**pay**sher er**goo**lyer	garfish
pescadinha	pershker**dhee**nyer	whiting
polvo	**poal**voo	octopus
robalo	roo**bhah**loo	sea bass
rodovalho	roodhoo**vah**lyoo	turbot
salmão (fumado)	sahl**mahng**ᵂ (foomah**dhoo**)	(smoked) salmon
santola	sahng**toller**	crab
sardinhas	ser**dee**nyersh	sardines
sável	**sah**vehl	shad
sururú	soo**roo**roo	a kind of mollusc (Braz.)

Here are some of the ways you may want the fish served:

baked	**no forno**	noo foarnoo
fried	**frito**	freetoo
grilled	**grelhado**	grerlyahdhoo
marinated	**de escabeche**	der ishkerbehsher
poached	**cozido [pochê]**	koozeedhoo [poshay]
sautéed	**salteado [sauté]**	sahlterahdhoo [soatay]
smoked	**fumado [defumado]**	foomahdhoo [dayfoo-mahdhoa]
steamed	**cozido a vapor**	koozeedhoo ah verpoar

Bacalhau (dried, salted cod) dishes are among the most famous Portuguese specialities. Here are the names of a few of the more common preparations you're likely to find:

bacalhau à brás
(berkerlyow ah brahz)

strips of dried cod fried with onions and potatoes, cooked in beaten eggs

bacalhau à Gomes de Sá
(berkerlyow ah goamersh der sah)

dried cod with olives, garlic, onions, parsley and hard-boiled eggs

bacalhau podre
(berkerlyow poadrer)

a baked dish, in which layers of cod, fried in butter, alternate with layers of sliced, fried potatoes; topped with breadcrumbs and grated cheese

bacalhau com leite de coco
(bahkahlyow kawng layti dee koakoa)

cod stewed in coconut milk (Braz.)

And try one of these specialities:

caldeirada
(kahldayrahdher)

several kinds of fish simmered with onions, potatoes, and olive oil

lulas recheadas
(loolersh rersherahdhersh)

squid cooked with a stuffing of egg yolk, minced ham, onion and tomato sauce

moqueca de peixe
(mokkaykah dèe payshi)

stew made of fish, shellfish or shrimp with coconut milk, *dendê* oil (yellow palm oil) and other seasoning (Braz.)

vatapá
(vahtahpah)

fish and shrimp (dried and fresh) in paste made of rice flour or breadcrumbs, coconut milk, *dendê* oil, peanuts, cashew nuts and other seasonings (Braz.)

Meat

In Portugal, *bife* (**bee**fer—from the English word beef) turns out to be the word for steak—even when referring to veal, pork or fish. Veal *bifes* taste better than beef *bifes* most of the time. And you may try some lamb *costeletas* (chops), which are delicious in Portugal.

EATING OUT

I'd like some…	Queria…	kerreeer
beef	**carne de vaca**	kahrner der vahker
lamb	**borrego [carneiro]**	boorraygoo [kahrnayroa]
pork	**porco**	poarkoo
veal	**carne de vitela**	kahrner der vittehler
bife	beefer	steak
borrego [carneiro]	boorraygoo [kahrnayroa]	lamb
assado	erssahdhoo	roast lamb
cabrito	kerbreetoo	kid
carne de vaca	kahrner der vahker	beef
assada	erssahdher	roast beef
cozida	koozeedher	boiled beef
carneiro	kerrnayroo	mutton
carnes frias	kahrnersh freeersh	cold cuts
chouriço	shoareessoo	sausage
costeleta	kooshterlaytersh	chop, cutlet
fiambre [presunto]	fyahngbrer [prayzoong-toa]	gammon (ham)
fígado	feegerdhoo	liver
leitão	laytahng^w	suckling pig
língua	leenggwer	tongue
porco	poarkoo	pork
assado	erssahdoo	roast pork
presunto	prayzoongtoo	smoked ham
cru	kroo	raw ham
rins	reengsh	kidneys
salsicha	sahlseesher	sausage
toucinho fumado	toasseenyoo foomahdhoo	bacon
vitela	vittehler	veal

bife na frigideira
(**bee**fer ner frizhi**dda**yrer)
beefsteak fried in butter, white wine and garlic, served with ham and fried bread

carne de porco à
Alentejana
(**kah**rner der **poar**koo er erlayngter**zhah**ner)
chopped pork cooked with clams, tomatoes and onions

carne de sol com feijão verde (**kahr**ni dee sol kawng fayz**hahng**ᵛ **vay**rdi)	meat dried in the sun (jerk) and beans (Braz.)
cozido à Portuguesa (koo**zee**dhoo er poortoo**gay**zer)	boiled beef, gammon(ham), smoked sausage, rice and vegetables
churrasco misto (shoo**rrah**skoa **mees**toa)	mixed barbecue (beef, sausage and pork) (Braz.)
feijoada (fayz**wah**dhah)	Brazil's national dish. Black beans cooked with bacon, dried and salted pork, jerk and sausage. You eat it with rice, slices of orange and *farofa*, manioc flour roasted in butter or oil.
rojões à moda do Minho (roo**zhawng**ᵛsh ah **mo**dher der **mee**nyoo)	chopped pork, marinated in dry white wine with onions and herbs and then fried
sarapatel (sahrahpah**tehl**)	a stew of pork or mutton innards and blood (Braz.)

How do you like your meat?

English	Portuguese	Pronunciation
baked	**no forno**	noo **foar**noo
baked in parchment	**assada em alumínio**	er**ssah**dher ayng erloo**mee**nyoo
boiled	**cozida**	koo**zee**dher
braised	**estufada**	ishtoo**fah**dher
fried	**frita**	**free**ter
grilled	**grelhada**	grerl**yah**dher
roasted	**assada**	er**ssah**dher
sautéed	**salteada [sauté]**	sahlt**yah**dher [**soa**tay]
stewed	**guisada [estufada]**	gizz**ah**dher [aystoo**fah**dhah]
underdone (rare)	**meio crua**	**may**oo **kroo**er
medium	**média [ao ponto]**	**meh**dhyer [ow **pawng**toa
well-done	**bem passada**	bayng per**ssah**dher

Game and fowl

In both Portugal and Brazil, chicken is a favourite dish, prepared in dozens of ways. The Portuguese may surprise you with the great choice of game and fowl dishes available in various regions.

I'd like some game.	Queria caça.	kerreeer kahsser
capão	kerpahngʷ	capon
codorniz [codorna]	koodhorneesh [koddoar-nah]	quail
coelho	kwaylyoo	rabbit
faisão	fighzahngʷ	pheasant
frango	frahnggoo	chicken
galinha	gerleenyer	stewing chicken
galinha assada	gerleenyer erssahdher	roast chicken
coxa/perna de galinha	koasher/pehrner der gerleenyer	chicken leg
peito de galinha	paytoo der gerleenyer	chicken breast
galinhola	gerlinyoller	woodcock
ganso	gahngsoo	goose
javali	zherverlee	wild boar
lebre	lehbrer	hare
pato	pahtoo	duck
perdiz	perrdeesh	partridge
perú	perroo	turkey
pombo	pawngboo	pigeon
veado	vyahdhoo	venison

arroz de frango (erroash der frahnggoo)	fried chicken with white wine, ham and rice in a casserole
coelho assado (kwaylyoo erssahdhoo)	roast rabbit with onions, white wine and seasoning
galeto com polenta (gahlaytoa kawng pollayngtah)	fried chicken with polenta (Braz.)
frango na Púcara (frahnggoo ner pookerrer)	chicken stewed in Port wine and cognac, then fried with almonds cooked in wine sauce
pato no tucupí (pahtoa noa tookoopee)	roast duck with *tucupí*, a manioc juice (Braz.)
xinxim de galinha (sheengsheeng dee gahleenyah)	chicken cooked in a sauce of dried shrimp, peanuts and parsley (Braz.)

Vegetables

What vegetables do you recommend?	Que legumes me aconselha?	ker lergoomersh mer erkawngsaylyer
aspargos	ahspahrgoas	asparagus
abóbora	erbobboorer	marrow
agriões	ergryawngᵛsh	watercress
aipo	ighpoo	celery
alcachofra	ahlkershoafrer	artichoke
alface	ahlfahsser	lettuce
alho	ahlyoo	garlic
alho porro	ahlyoo poaroo	leeks
batatas	bertahtersh	potatoes
batata doce	bertahter doasser	sweet potato (Braz.)
berinjela	berreengzhehler	eggplant (aubergine)
brócolo [brócoli]	brokkooloo [brokkoali]	broccoli
beterraba	berterrrahbher	beetroot
cebolas	serboalersh	onions
cenouras	sernoarersh	carrots
chicória	shikkorryer	endive (US chicory)
cogumelos	koogoomehloosh	mushrooms
couve	koaver	cabbage
couve-flor	koaver floar	cauliflower
ervilhas	errveelyersh	peas
espargos	ishpahrgoosh	asparagus
favas	fahversh	broad beans
feijão	fayzhahngʷ	red or black beans
feijão verde	fayzhahngʷ vayrder	haricot beans
funcho	foongshoo	fennel
grão	grahngʷ	chick peas
legumes mistos	lergoomersh meeshtoosh	mixed vegetables
lentilhas	layngteelyersh	lentils
milho doce	meelyoo doasser	sweet corn
palmito	pahlmeetoa	heart of palm (Braz.)
pepino	perpeenoo	cucumber
pepinos pequenos	perpeenoosh perkaynoosh	gherkins
pimentos doces	pimmayngtoosh doassersh	sweet peppers
quiabo	kyahbhoa	okra (Braz.)
rabanetes	rerbernaytersh	radishes
repolho	rerpoalyoo	savoy cabbage
salada mista	serlahdher meeshter	mixed salad
salsa	sahlser	parsley
tomates	toomahtersh	tomatoes
trufas	troofersh	truffles
vagens	vahzhahngᵛsh	haricot beans
xuxú	shooshoo	a type of rutabaga (Braz.)

And if you're touring in Brazil, try one of these delicious vegetable dishes:

acarajé (ahkahrah**zheh**)	grated beans fried in *dendê* (palm) oil, served with pepper sauce, onions and shrimp
tutú à mineira (tootoo ah min**nay**rah)	a dish made of beans, manioc flour, pork, cabbage, fried eggs and browned rashers of lard

Cheese

Portuguese cheeses are usually a mixture of sheep's and goat's milk, or cow's and goat's milk. Brazil also produces some cheese, which you're expected to eat as a dessert, accompanied by preserves or sweets—*goiabada,* a paste made of guava, for instance. A cheeseboard is seldom served in Portuguese or Brazilian restaurants.

I'd like some cheese.   **Queria queijo.**   kerree**er** kay**zhoo**

creamy	Queijo da Serra, Azeitão, Évora, Castelo Branco, Serpa, Requeijão (a Brazilian cheese produced in Minas Gerais)
goat's milk cheese	Cabreiro (must be eaten fresh), Queijo de Minas (Brazilian, delicious with *goiabada*)
cow's milk cheese	São João, São Jorge, Ilha (from the Azores Islands), Queijo do Sertão (Brazilian)

EATING OUT

Fruit

Do you have fresh fruit?	**Tem fruta fresca?**	tayng frooter frayshker
I'd like a (fresh) fruit cocktail.	**Queria uma salada de fruta (fresca).**	kerreeer oomer serlahdher der frooter (**frayshker**)
abacaxí	ahbahkahshee	pineapple (Braz.)
alperches	ahlpehrshersh	apricots
ameixas	ermayshersh	plums
ameixas passas [secas]	ermayshersh pahssersh [**saykahss**]	prunes
amêndoas	ermayngdwersh	almonds
amoras	ermorrersh	mulberries
ananás	ernernahsh	pineapple
avelãs	erverlahngsh	hazelnuts
banana	bernahner	banana
caqui	kahkee	persimmon (Braz.)
castanhas	kershtahnyersh	chestnuts
cerejas	serrayzhersh	cherries
damascos	dahmahskoass	apricots (Braz.)
figos	feegoosh	figs
framboesas	frahngbwayzersh	raspberries
goiaba	goyahbah	guava (Braz.)
laranja	lerrahngzher	orange
lima	leemer	lime
limão	limmahngw	lemon
limão verde	limmahngw vayrdi	lime (Braz.)
maçã	merssahng	apple
mamão	mahmahngw	papaw (Braz.)
maracujá	mahrahkoozhah	passion-fruit (Braz.)
melancia	merlahngseeer	watermelon
melão	merlahngw	melon
morangos	moorahnggoosh	strawberries
nêsperas	nayshperrersh	crab apple
nozes	nozzersh	walnuts
passa de uva	pahssersh der oover	sultanas/raisins
pêra	payrer	pear
pêssego	payssergoo	peach
tâmaras	tahngmerrersh	dates
tangerinas	tahngzherreenersh	tangerines
toranja	torrahngzher	grapefruit
uvas	ooversh	grapes
umbu	oongboo	a tropical fruit (Braz.)

Dessert

Cakes, custards and sweets—usually made of egg yolks (Portugal) or grated coconut (Brazil)—are part of every meal. You'll probably find them a bit too sweet; if so, try a Portuguese ice-cream (*gelado* in Portugal, called *sorvete* in Brazil). They're delicious!

I'd like a dessert, please.	**Queria uma sobremesa, por favor.**	kerreeer oomer soobrermayzer poor fervoar
Something light, please.	**Algo de ligeiro [Algo leve], por favor.**	ahlgoo der lizhayroo [ahlgoa lehvi] poor fervoar
Just a small portion.	**Uma dose pequena, por favor.**	oomer dozzer perkayner poor fervoar
Nothing more, thanks.	**É tudo, obrigado.**	eh toodhoo oobriggahdhoo

If you are not sure...

What do you have for dessert?	**O que tem de sobremesa?**	oo ker tayng der soobrermayzer
What do you recommend?	**O que me aconselha?**	oo ker mer erkawngsaylyer

biscoitos	biskawngtoosh	biscuits (cookies)
bolo	boaloo	cake
gelado [sorvete]	gerlahdhoo [soarvayti]	ice-cream
de baunilha	der bowneelyer	vanilla
de chocolate	der shookoolahter	chocolate
de maracujá	dee mahrahkoozhah	passion-fruit
de morango	der moorahnggoo	strawberry
pudim flã	poodheeng flahng	egg custard in a caramel sauce
pudim de laranja	poodheeng der lerrahngzher	orange-flavoured custard
pudim de ovos	poodheeng der ovvoosh	egg pudding
arroz doce (ahrroas doassi)		rice pudding
baba de môça (bahbhah dee moassah)		a sweet made of sugar, syrup, coconut milk and cinnamon (Braz.)
cocada (kokkahdhah)		a sweet made of grated coconut (Braz.)

doce de abóbora
(doassi dee ahbobborrah)

pumpkin-paste cake with coconut (Braz.)

farófias
(ferroffyersh)

beaten egg whites, cooked in sweetened milk, topped with cinnamon and egg custard

goiabada
(gawngʸahbahdah)

a thick paste made of guavas (Braz.)

The bill

I'd like to pay.	**Queria pagar.**	kerreeer pergahr
We'd like to pay separately.	**Queríamos pagar cada um separadamente.**	kerreeermoosh pergahr kerdher oong serperrahdhermayngter
You've made a mistake in this bill, I think.	**Creio que se enganou na conta.**	krayoo ker ser aynggernoaner kawngter
What is this amount for?	**A que corresponde esta importância?**	er ker koorrershpawngder ehshter eengpoortahngsyer
Is service included?	**O serviço está incluído?**	oo serrveessoo ishtah eengklweedhoo
Is everything included?	**Está tudo incluído?**	ishtah toodhoo eengklweedhoo
Do you accept traveller's cheques?	**Aceita cheques de viagem?**	erssayter shehkersh der vyahzhayng
Thank you, this is for you.	**Obrigado, isto é para si.**	oabriggahdhoo ishtoo eh perrer see
Keep the change.	**Guarde o troco.**	gwahrder oo troakoo
That was a very good meal.	**A refeição estava muito boa.**	er rerfayssahngʷ ishtahver moongʸtoo boaer
We enjoyed it, thank you.	**Apreciámos [Gostámos], obrigado.**	erprerssyahmoosh [goastahmoass] oobriggahdhoo

---

SERVIÇO INCLUÍDO
SERVICE INCLUDED

Complaints

But perhaps you'll have something to complain about:

That's not what I ordered. I asked for…	**Não é o que eu encomendei. Eu pedi…**	nahng^w eh oo ker ehoo ayngkoomayngday. ehoo perdhee
May I change this?	**Pode trocar isto?**	podher trookahr ishtoo
The meat is…	**A carne está…**	er kahrner ishtah
overdone	**passada demais**	perssahdher dermighsh
underdone	**mal passada**	mahl perssahdher
too rare	**muito crua**	moong^ytoo krooer
too tough	**dura demais**	doorer dermighsh
This is too…	**Isto está muito…**	ishtoo ishtah moong^ytoo
bitter/salty	**amargo/salgado**	ermahrgoo/sahlgahdhoo
sweet	**doce**	doasser
The food is cold.	**A comida está fria.**	er koomeedher ishtah freeer
This isn't fresh.	**Isto não é fresco.**	ishtoo nahng^w eh frayshkoo
What's taking you so long?	**Porque demora tanto?**	poorker dermorrer tahngtoo
Where are our drinks?	**Esqueceu-se de nos trazer as bebidas?**	ishkerssehoo ser der noosh trerzayr ersh berbheedhersh
This isn't clean.	**Isto não está limpo.**	ishtoo nahng^w ishtah leengpoo
Would you ask the head waiter to come over?	**Pode chamar o Chefe de Mesa [Gerente], por favor?**	podher shermahr oo shehfer der mayzer [zhayrayngti] poor fervoar

Drinks

Aperitifs

The Portuguese like to sip a before-dinner *vermute* (verr-*moo*ter—vermouth), you'll find that some prefer a light Porto or a *Moscatel de Setúbal* as an aperitif; Brazilians will rather have a *batida* (sugar cane rum, lime and ice), a beer or a gin and tonic.

Wine

Climatic conditions in Portugal account for the variety in the nature and quality of the wine. Some wine-producing regions are classified and controlled by law, because of the distinguishing characteristics of their wines. This goes for the Douro Valley in northern Portugal (Port wine), and the districts of Dão, Bucelas and Colares.

Wine production in the Douro Valley dates back to the Crusades. However the wine which today we call Port had its origin several centuries later. In 1678, two Englishmen, having just bought the output of a monastery's vineyard, puzzled over how to ship it back to Britain in order that it might arrive in good condition. They hit upon the idea of adding a little brandy to each of the casks. Thus the famous Port wine was born.

To ensure the integrity of the wine, the Portuguese Port Wine Institute closely overlooks production and shipment. Not only is the growing area for Port wine strictly limited, but constant checks are made on the wine leaving the country to monitor colour, bouquet and quality. In a particularly good year, the wine will be granted a vintage.

The Portuguese seem to prefer the drier, lighter types as aperitifs or dessert wines. You'll notice that a much more popular wine than Port is the light, white *Moscatel* from the Setúbal area, south of Lisbon. It's often drunk before meals.

The *vinhos verdes* (red, rosé or white) are called *verdes* (green) because the grapes, though ripe, are sour and contain little sugar. They have a low percentage of alcohol and originate from the Minho region, northwest of Portugal.

According to a Portuguese law, hotels, *pousadas* and boarding-houses are expected to offer guests who order fixed-price meals 3/5 litre of their house wine (*vinho da casa*—**vee**nyoo der **kah**zer).

Brazilian wines are produced in the southern part of the country. This region turns out some good red wines, and white wines too. Brazilians however—probably because of the hot climate—prefer beer or some of their exotic and refreshing drinks.

Type of wine	Examples	Accompanies
sweet white wine	*Moscatel, Carcavelos, Favaios* (similar to muscatel) *Madeira* (Sercial)	all kind of desserts, sweets; goes well with custards; *Moscatel* is often taken before meals
sweet red wine	*Madeira* (Malmsey, Bual), *Douro* (Port wine)	dessert and sweets; as an aperitif; in a sauce, they give a delicious taste to the meat
dry and light white wine	*Almeirim, Dão,* most of the white-type *vinhos verdes, Bucelas, Alcobaça, Oeiras, Colares, Douro* (Porca de Murça, Cacho de Oyro Pérola)	fish, seafood, appetizers, cheese dishes
rosé (rosado)	*Pinhel,* rosé-type *vinhos verdes*	poultry; cold dishes
light-bodied red wine	*Amaral, Gaeiras,* all the red-type *vinhos verdes, Douro* (Douro Clarete, Palhete)	poultry; meat
full-bodied red wine	*Periquita, Lagoa, Colares* (Serradayres), *Dão, Bairrada*	meat and game
sparkling wine	*Espumante* (Portuguese champagne); most of the *vinhos verdes, Bairrada*—especially renowned are the *vinhos espumantes naturais* from the *Caves da Raposeira*	desserts and sweets; as an aperitif

EATING OUT

I'd like a…of…	**Queria…de…**	kerreeer…der
glass	**um copo**	oong koppoo
carafe	**um jarro**	oong zhahrroo
half bottle	**uma meia garrafa**	oomer mayer gerrrahfer
bottle	**uma garrafa**	oomer gerrrahfer
litre	**um litro**	oong leetroo

I want a bottle of white/red wine.	**Queria uma garrafa de vinho branco/ tinto.**	kerreee' oomer gerrrahfer der veenyoo brahngkoo/ teengtoo
Do you have open wine?	**Tem vinho da casa?**	tayng veenyoo dah kahzer
Please bring me another bottle.	**Queria outra garrafa.**	kerreeer aotrer gerrrahfer
Where does this wine come from?	**Donde vem este vinho?**	dawngder vayng ayshter veenyoo
What is the name of this wine?	**Qual é o nome deste vinho?**	kwahl eh oo nommer dayshter veenyoo
How old is this wine?	**Quantos anos tem este vinho?**	kwahngtoosh ernoosh tayng ayshter veenyoo

red	**tinto**	teengtoo
white	**branco**	brahngkoo
rosé	**rosé/rosado**	rozzay/roozahdhoo
dry	**seco**	saykoo
sweet	**doce**	doasser
light	**ligeiro [leve]**	lizhayroo [lehvi]
full-bodied	**encorpado [com buquê]**	ayngkoarpahdhoo [kawng bookay]
sparkling	**espumante**	ishpoomahngter
chilled	**fresco**	frayshkoo
at room temperature	**à temperatura ambiente**	ah tayngperrahtoorer ahngbyayngter

Other alcoholic drinks

Bars and hotels in major tourist centres usually have a good stock of foreign and domestic beer, wine and liquor. Off the beaten track, brands will be largely local. You may want to sample a Portuguese ale like *Sagres* or even the local *aguardente,* an explosive raw white spirit. In Brazil, beware of the *cachaça,* a very strong rum made from sugar cane.

aperitif	um aperitivo	oong erperritteevoo
beer	uma cerveja	oomer serrvayzher
brandy	um conhaque	oong konnyahker
raw brandy	uma aguardente	oomer ahgwerrdayngter
cider	uma sidra	oomer seedrer
cognac	um conhaque	oong konnyahker
cordial	um cordial	oong kordyahl
gin	uma genebra [um gim]	oomer zhernehbrer [oong zheeng]
gin-fizz	um gin-fizz	oong zheeng feez
gin and tonic	uma genebra [um gim] com água tónica	oomer zhernehbrer [oong zheeng] kawng ahgwer tonnikker
liqueur	um licor	oong likkoar
Port	vinho do Porto	veenyoo doo poartoo
rum	um rum [um ron/ uma cachaça]	oong roong [oong rawng/ oomer kahshahssah]
Scotch	um uísque	oong wishker
sherry	um xerez	oong shehraysh
vermouth	um vermute	oong verrmooter
vodka	uma vodka	oomer vodker
whisky	um uísque	oong wishker
and soda	com água de sifão [com soda]	kawng ahgwer der siffahng^w [kawng sodder]

glass	um copo	oong koppoo
bottle	uma garrafa	oomer gerrrahfer
neat (straight)	puro	pooroo
on the rocks	com gelo	kawng zhayloo

If you'd like to sip a brandy after dinner, try a Portuguese *conhaque* like *Borges* or *Constantino*. You may also sample a local liqueur named *Tríplice* or a *Barros* (grape brandy).

I'd like to try a glass of..., please.	Queria provar um copo de..., por favor.	kerreeer proovahr oong koppoo der...poor fervoar
Are there any local specialities?	Há especialidades regionais?	ah ishperssyahlidhahdhersh rerzhyoonighsh
Please bring me a glass of Borges.	Traga-me um Borges, por favor.	trahger mer oong borgeesh poor fervoar

Batida, a very exotic Brazilian speciality, is an explosive cocktail. It may seem most palatable to non-Brazilians, but watch out for the effects! *Batida*'s basic ingredient is the *cachaça*, a quite strong sugar-cane rum. Add some (tropical) fruit juice, sugar and ice, and you'll have a *batida*.

batida de cajú
(bahteedah dee kahzhoo)
cachaça, cashew juice, sugar and ice

batida de maracujá
(bahteedah dee mahrahkoozhah)
cachaça, passion-fruit juice, sugar and ice

caipirinha
(kighpirreenyah)
lime juice, *cachaça,* sugar and ice

> **SAÚDE**
> (seroodher)
> CHEERS!

Other beverages

I'd like a...	Queria...	kerreeer
(hot) chocolate	um chocolate (quente)	oong shookoolahter (kayngter)
coffee	um café	oong kerfeh
black	puro [preto]	pooroo [praytoa]
with cream	com nata [creme]	kawng nahter [kraymer]
espresso coffee	um expresso [cafèzinho]	oong ishprehssoo [kahfehzeenyoa]
iced coffee	um café gelado	oong kerfeh zherlahdhoo
fruit juice	um sumo [suco]	oong soomoo [sookoa]
	de frutas	der frootersh
apple	de maçã	der merssahng
grapefruit	de toranja	der torrahngzher
lemon	de limão	der limmahng^w
orange	de laranja	der lerrahngzher
pineapple	de ananás [abacaxí]	der ernernahsh [ahbahkahshee]
tomato	de tomate	der toomahter
lemonade	uma limonada	oomer limoonahdher
milkshake	um batido [um milkshake]	oong berteedhoo [oong milkshaykee]
mineral water	água mineral	ahgwer minnerrahl

orangeade	**uma laranjada**	oomer lerrahng**zhah**dher
lemon squash (soda pop)	**uma limonada**	oomer limm**onnah**dhah
tea	**chá**	shah
with milk	**com leite**	kawng **lay**ter
with lemon	**com limão**	kawng lim**mahng**ʷ
iced tea	**um chá gelado**	oong shah zherl**ah**dhoo
tonic water	**uma água tónica**	oomer **ah**gwer **t**onnikker

Note: Drinking tap water is not recommended, especially in Brazil.

Refreshing drinks

Brazilians are very fond of cool and refreshing drinks (*refrescos*—ray**frays**koas). Some are very exotic, some quite sweet. Have a try!

água de côco	ahgwah dee **ko**akoa	coconut milk
caldo de cana	kahl**d**oa dee **kah**nah	sugar cane juice
Cuba libre	koob**h**ah **lee**bri	rum and coke
guaraná	gwahrah**n**ah	a soft drink flavoured with a tropical fruit
milkshake	milk**shay**kee	milkshake
de chocolate	dee shokk**ol**lahti	chocolate-flavoured
de café	dee kah**feh**	coffee-flavoured
de morango	dee moor**ahng**goo	strawberry-flavoured
suco de abacaxí	sookoo dee ahb**h**ahkah-shee	pineapple juice
suco de maracujá	sookoo dee mahrah-koo**zh**ah	passion-fruit juice

Coffee

Drunk anytime of the day—or night—Brazilian *cafèzinho* (a strong, espresso-type coffee) is served black with a lot of sugar to make it less bitter-tasting. Never add milk or cream when it's offered to you: your hosts might think you don't like the way they prepare it.

| I'd like a coffee. | **Queria um cafèzinho.** | kerr**eee**er oong kahfeh-**zee**nyoa |

Eating light—Snacks

You may not feel like having a big meal in a restaurant and may just want a quick bite at a *casa de lanche* (Brazil), also called snack-bar in both Portugal and Brazil. Since most of the snacks are on display, you won't need to say much more than:

I'll have one of those, please.	**Tomo um destes, por favor.**	tommoo oong dayshtersh poor fervoar
Please give me a/some...	**Dê-me..., por favor.**	day mer... poor fervoar
biscuits (Br.)	**uns biscoitos**	oongsh bishkawng⋎toosh
bread	**pão**	pahngʷ
butter	**manteiga**	mahngtayger
cake	**um bolo**	oong boaloo
candy	**rebuçados [balas]**	rerboossahdhoosh [bahlahss]
chocolate (bar)	**(uma barra de) chocolate**	(oomer bahrrer der) shookoolahter
cookies	**uns biscoitos**	oongsh bishkawng⋎toosh
hamburger	**um hamburgo [um hamburger]**	oong ahngboorgoo [oong ahngboorgehr]
heart of palm salad	**salada de palmito**	sahlahdhah dee pahlmeetoa
hot dog	**um cachorro quente**	oong kershoarroo kayngter
ice-cream	**um gelado [sorvete]**	oong zherlahdhoo [soarvayti]
pastry	**uns bolos [doces]**	oongsh boaloosh [doassiss]
pie	**um pastel**	oong pershtehl
meat pie	**pastel de carne**	pershtehl der kahrner
shrimp pie	**pastel de camarões**	pershtehl der kahmahrawng⋎s (Braz.)
tuna pie	**uma empada de atum**	oomer ayngpahdhah der ertoong
roll	**um pãozinho**	oong pahngʷzeenyoo
sandwich	**uma [um] sanduíche**	oomer [oong] sahngdweesher
(fried) shrimp	**camarões (fritos)**	kahmahrawng⋎s (freetoass)
sweets	**rebuçados [balas]**	rerboossahdhoosh [bahlahss]
toast	**uma torrada**	oomer toorrahdher
How much is that?	**Quanto custa isto?**	kwahngtoo kooshter ishtoo

Travelling around

Plane

Very brief—because at any airport or airline office you're
sure to find someone who speaks English.

Is there a flight to Madeira?	Há um voo para a Madeira?	ah oong **voaoo per**rer er merd**hay**rer
Is it a nonstop flight?	É voo directo?	eh **voa**oo dir**reh**too
When's the next plane to Faro?	A que horas parte o próximo avião para Faro?	er ker orrersh **pahr**ter oo **pros**simmoo ervyahng^w perrer **fah**roo
Do I have to change planes?	Tenho de mudar de avião?	**teh**nyoo der **mood**hahr der er**vyahng**^w
Can I make a connection to Porto?	Tenho ligação [conexão] para o Porto?	**teh**nyoo ligger**ssahng**^w [konneh**ksahng**^w] perrer oo **poar**too
I'd like a ticket to Lisbon.	Quero um bilhete [uma passagem] para Lisboa?	**keh**roo oong bil**lyay**ter [**oo**mah pah**ssah**zhayng] perrer lizh**boa**er
What's the fare to...?	Qual é o preço do bilhete [da passagem] para...?	kwahl eh oo **prays**soo doo bil**lyay**ter [dah pah**ssah**zhayng] **per**rer
single (one-way)	ida	**eed**her
return (roundtrip)	ida e volta	**eed**her i **vol**ter
What time does the plane take off?	A que horas parte o avião?	er ker orrersh **pahr**ter oo er**vyahng**^w
What time do I have to check in?	A que horas devo apresentar-me?	er ker orrersh **day**voo erprerzayng**tahr** mer
What's the flight number?	Qual é o número do voo?	kwahl eh oo **noo**merroo doo **voa**oo
At what time do we arrive?	A que horas chegamos?	er ker orrersh sherg**ah**moosh

CHEGADA ARRIVAL	**PARTIDA** DEPARTURE

Train

The Portuguese railway network is fast and trains generally run on time on the main lines. They offer first and second class seats. As fares are low, foreigners usually travel first class wherever possible. Early booking is advisable. For booking or inquiries, you should go to a travel agent.

Types of trains

automotora
(owtoomoatoarer)

Fast diesel-propelled train with two carriages only; early booking advisable.

correio
(koorrayoo)

Long-distance postal train; operates twice daily (morning and evening); also takes passengers.

internacional
(eengternáhssyoonahl)

A direct train; for a trip abroad you'll have to book a seat in advance, as one carriage only crosses the border.

Lusitania-Express
loozittahnyer
(aysprehss)

Luxury express; links Lisbon with Madrid; early booking advisable.

rápido
(rahpidhoo)

Direct train

Sud-Express
(sood aysprehss)

Comfortable luxury express (first class only); will take you from Lisbon to Paris in 24 hours.

TER
(tehr)

Diesel express, air-conditioned, supplementary fare required; runs from Lisbon to Madrid.

Long-distance bus

Long-distance bus and coach services are reasonably frequent, and cover most of the Portuguese provinces. In remote districts, though, local buses may run irregularly; they are often very crowded.

Note: Most of the phrases on the following pages can be used or adapted for bus travel.

To the railway station

Where's the railway station?	**Onde é a estação dos caminhos de ferro [estação ferroviária]?**	**awng**der eh er ishter**ssahng**ʷ doosh ker**mee**nyoosh der **feh**rroo [istah**ssahng**ʷ fehrroa**vyah**ryah]
Taxi, please!	**Táxi, por favor.**	**tah**ksi poor fer**voar**
Take me to the railway station.	**Conduza-me à estação dos caminhos de ferro [estação ferroviária].**	kawng**doo**zer mer ah ishter**ssahng**ʷ doosh ker**mee**nyoosh der **feh**rroo [istah**ssahng**ʷ fehrroa**vyah**ryah]
What's the fare?	**Quanto custa?**	**kwahng**too **koosh**ter

ENTRADA	ENTRANCE
SAÍDA	EXIT
ACESSO AOS CAIS	TO THE PLATFORMS

Where's the...?

Where is/are the...?	**Onde é/são...?**	**awng**der eh/sahngʷ
booking office	**a secção de reservas**	er sehk**sahng**ʷ der rer**zehr**versh
buffet	**o buffet**	oo boo**feh**
currency exchange office	**a agência de câmbio [o câmbio]**	ah er**zhayng**syer der **kahng**byoo [oo **kahng**byoa]
information office	**as informações**	ersh eengfoormer**ssawng**ʸ**sh**
left-luggage office (baggage check)	**o depósito da bagagem**	oo der**po**zzittoo der ber**gah**zhayng
lost-property (lost-and-found) office	**o depósito dos objectos perdidos**	oo der**po**zzittoo doosh oob**zheh**toosh per**dee**dhoosh
luggage lockers	**os cacifos [o depósito] de bagagem**	oosh ker**ssee**foosh [oo deh**po**zzittoa] der ber**gah**zhayng
news-stand	**o quiosque [a banca] de jornais**	oo **kyosh**ker [ah **bahng**kah] der zhoor**nighsh**
platform 7	**a linha 7**	er **lee**nyer 7
restaurant	**o restaurante**	oo restow**rahng**ter
ticket office	**a bilheteira**	er billyay**tay**rer
waiting-room	**a sala de espera**	er **sah**ler der ish**peh**rer

FOR TAXI, see page 27

Inquiries

When is the... train to Sagres?	**A que horas parte o... comboio* para Sagres?**	er ker orrersh **pahrter** oo... koamboyoo perrer sahgrersh
first/last/next	**primeiro/último/ próximo**	primmayroo/ooltimmoo/ prossimmoo
What time does the train for Braga leave?	**Quando parte o comboio* para Braga?**	kwahngdhoo pahrter oo koamboyoo perrer brahger
What's the fare to Faro?	**Quanto custa a passagem para Faro?**	kwahngtoo kooshter er perssahzhayng perrer fahroo
Is it a through train?	**É um comboio* directo?**	eh oong koamboyoo dirrehtoo
Will the train leave on time?	**O comboio* parte a horas [na hora]?**	oo koamboyoo pahrter er orrersh [nah orrah]
What time does the train arrive at Lisbon?	**A que horas chega o comboio* a Lisboa?**	er ker orrersh shayger oo koamboyoo er lizhbhoaer
Is there a dining-car on the train?	**O comboio* leva vagão-restaurante?**	oo koamboyoo lehver vergahng^w restowrahngter
Is there a sleeping-car on the train?	**O comboio* tem car-ruagem-cama [vagão-leito]?**	oo koamboyoo tayng kerr-wahzhayng kahmer [vahgahng^w laytoa]
Does the train stop at Coimbra?	**O comboio* pára em Coimbra?**	oo koamboyoo pahrer ayng kweengbrer
What platform does the train for Óbidos leave from?	**De que linha parte o comboio* para Óbidos?**	der ker leenyer pahrter oo koamboyoo perrer obbidhoosh
What platform does the train from... arrive at?	**A que plataforma chega o comboio* de...?**	ah ker plahterformer shayger oo koamboyoo der
I'd like to buy a timetable.	**Queria comprar um horário.**	kerreeer kawngprahr oong oorahryoo

---

* In Brazil: **trem** (trayng).

É um comboio [trem] directo.	It's a through train.
Tem de mudar em...	You have to change at...
Mude em... e apanhe [pegue] um comboio [trem] local.	Change at... and get a local train.
Cais... fica...	Platform... is...
além/em cima	over there/upstairs
à esquerda/à direita	on the left/on the right
Há um comboio [trem] para... às...	There's a train to... at...
O seu comboio [trem] parte do cais	Your train will leave from platform...
O comboio [trem] tem um atraso de... minutos	There'll be a delay of...minutes.

Tickets

I want a ticket to Faro.	Queria um bilhete [uma passagem] para Faro.	kerreeer oong billyayter [oomah pahssahzhayng] perrer fahroo
single (one-way)	ida	eedher
return (roundtrip)	ida e volta	eedher i volter
first class	primeira classe	primmayrer klahsser
second class	segunda classe	sergoonder klahsser
Isn't it half price for the boy/girl?	A criança não paga meio-preço?	er kryahngsser nahng^w pahger mayoo prayssoo

Primeira ou segunda classe?	First or second class?
Ida ou ida e volta?	Single or return (one-way or roundtrip)?
Quantos anos tem ele/ela?	How old is he/she?*

* In Portugal, children up to the age of 4 travel free, those between 4 and 12 pay half fare. In Brazil children up to the age of 12 pay half fare.

All aboard

Is this the right platform for the train to Faro?	**É este o cais do combóio* para Faro?**	eh **aysh**ter oo **kighsh** doo koam**boy**oo **perr**er **fah**roo
Is this the train to Madrid?	**É este o comboio* para Madrid?**	eh **aysh**ter oo koam**boy**oo **perr**er mer**dreed**
Excuse me. May I get by?	**Com licença. Posso passar?**	kawng li**ssayng**ser. **poss**oo per**ssahr**
Is this seat taken?	**Este lugar está ocupado?**	**aysh**ter **loo**gahr ish**tah** oakoo**pah**dhoo

---

PROIBIDO FUMAR
NO SMOKING

I think that's my seat.	**Creio que esse é o meu lugar.**	**kray**oo ker **ayss**er eh oo **meh**oo **loo**gahr
Would you let me know before we get to Coimbra?	**Pode avisar-me quando chegarmos [chegaremos] a Coimbra?**	**podh**er ervi**zzahr** mer **kwahng**doo sher**gahr**-moosh [shaygah**ray**moass] er **kween**gbrer
What station is this?	**Que estação é esta?**	ker ishter**ssahng**⁓ eh **ehsh**ter
How long does the train stop here?	**Quanto tempo pára o comboio* aqui?**	**kwahng**too **tayng**poo **pah**rer oo koam**boy**oo er**kee**
When do we get to Lisbon?	**Quando chegamos a Lisboa?**	**kwahng**doo sher**gah**-moosh er lizh**boa**er

Sometime on the journey the ticket collector (*o revisor* [*cobrador*]—oo revi**zzoar** [kobrah**doar**]) will come around and say: "*Bilhetes* [*Passagens*], *por favor!*" (Tickets, please).

Eating

Some Portuguese trains have a dining-car in which you can get a full meal. If the train is crowded there may be two sittings. Table wine comes with the price of the meal, though superior vintages cost extra.

* In Brazil: **trem** (trayng).

| Where's the dining-car? | **Onde está o vagão-restaurante?** | awngder ishtah oo vergahng^w rershtow-rahngter |
| First/Second sitting, please. | **Primeiro/Segundo serviço, por favor.** | primmayroo/sergoongdoo serrveessoo poor fervoar |

Sleeping

Are there any free compartments in the sleeping-car?	**Há compartimentos vazios no vagão--cama [vagão--leito]?**	ah kawngperrtimmayngtoosh verzeeoosh noo vergahng^w kahmer [vahgahng^w laytoa]
Where's the sleeping-car?	**Onde está o vagão--cama [vagão--leito]?**	awngder ishtah oo vergahng^w kahmer [vahgahng^w laytoa]
Where's my berth?	**Onde é a minha cama?**	awngder eh er meenyer kahmer
Compartments 18 and 19, please.	**Compartimentos 18 e 19, por favor.**	kawngperrtimmayngtoosh 18 ee 19 poor fervoar
I'd like a lower berth.	**Queria uma cama mais abaixo.**	kerreeer oomer kahmer mighsh erbighshoo
Would you make up our berths?	**Pode fazer as nossas camas?**	podher ferzayr ersh nossersh kahmersh
Would you call me at 7 o'clock?	**Pode acordar-me às 7 horas?**	podher erkoordahr mer ahsh 7 orrersh
Would you bring me some coffee in the morning?	**Pode trazer-me café, de manhã?**	podher trerzayrmer oo kerfeh der mernyahng

Baggage and porters

Porter!	**Bagageiro [Carregador]!**	bergerzhayroo [kahrraygahdoar]
Can you help me with my bags?	**Pode ajudar-me?**	podher erzhoodahhr mer
Please put them down here.	**Deixe-as aqui, por favor.**	daysher ersh erkee poor fervoar
Can I register these bags?	**Posso despachar estas malas?**	possoo dershpershahr ehshtersh mahlersh

FOR PORTERS, see also page 24

TRAVELING AROUND

Lost!

We hope you'll have no need for the following phrases on
your trip... but just in case:

Where's the lost-property (lost-and-found) office?	Onde está o depósito dos objectos perdidos?	awngder ishtah oo derpozzittoo doosh oobzhehtoosh perrdeedhoosh
I've lost my...	Perdi o meu/a minha...	perrdee oo mehoo/er meenyer
this morning yesterday	esta manhã ontem	ehshter mernyahng awngtayng
I lost it in...	Perdi-o/a em...	perrdee oo/er ayng
It's very valuable.	Tem muito valor.	tayng moong{v}too verloar

Underground (subway)

The *Metropolitano* in Lisbon has two main lines which join
at Pombal Square. The fare is the same irrespective of the
distance you travel. A very popular run is from the Avenida
da Liberdade to Campo Pequeno's bullring, in the outskirts
of Lisbon.

The underground runs from 6.10 a.m. to 1 a.m.

An underground system is being built in the Brazilian cities
of São Paulo and Rio.

Where's the nearest underground station?	Onde fica a mais próxima estação de metropolitano [metrô]?	awngder feeker er mighsh prossimmer ishterssahng{w} der mertroopoolittahnoo [mehtroa]
Does this train go to...?	Este combóio [trem] vai a...?	ayshter koamboyoo [trayng] vigh er
Where do I change for...?	Onde devo mudar para...?	awngder dayvoo moodhahr perrer
Is the next station ...?	A próxima estação é...?	er prossimmer ishterssahng{w} eh

Bus—Tram (streetcar)

Some buses board through the front door, others through the rear. Since there is no way of predicting, just look for the sign *Entrada* over one of the doors. (*Saída* means exit.)

I'd like a runabout ticket/a booklet of tickets.	**Queria um passe/ um abono, por favor.**	kerr**ee**er oong **pah**sser/ oong erb**hoa**noo poor fer**voar**
Where can I get a bus to the beach?	**Onde posso apanhar um autocarro* para a praia?**	awng**der** p**osso**o erper**nyahr** oong owtokk**ah**rroo perrer er pr**igh**er
What bus do I take for the University?	**Que autocarro* apanho para a Universidade?**	ker owtokk**ah**rroo erp**ah**nyoo perrer er oonivverrsid**hah**dher
Where's the...?	**Onde fica...?**	awng**der** f**ee**ker
bus stop	**a paragem dos autocarros [a parada de ônibus]**	er perr**ah**zhayng doosh owtokk**ah**rroosh [ah pah-**rah**dah di o**an**ibhoos]
terminus	**o terminus [ponto final]**	oo tehrm**inn**oosh [p**awng**toa f**inn**ahl]
When is the... bus to Belém?	**A que horas parte o... autocarro* para Belém?**	er ker **orr**ersh p**ahr**ter oo...owtokk**ah**rroo perrer berl**ayng**
first/last/next	**primeiro/último/ próximo**	prim**mayr**roo/**ool**timmoo/ pr**oss**immoo
How often do the buses to the town centre run?	**De quantos em quantos minutos é o autocarro* para a cidade?**	der kw**ahng**toosh ayng kw**ahng**toosh minn**oo**toosh eh oo owtokk**ah**rroo perrer er sid**hah**dher
How much is the fare to...?	**Quanto custa o bilhete [a passa- gem] para...?**	kw**ahng**too k**oosh**ter oo bill**yay**ter [ah pahssah-hayng] perrer
Do I have to change buses?	**Devo mudar de autocarro*?**	d**ay**voo mood**hahr** der owtokk**ah**rroo
Will you tell me when to get off?	**Pode dizer-me quando devo descer?**	p**odh**er dizz**ayr** mer kw**ahng**doo d**ay**voo derss**ayr**

* In Brazil: **ônibus** (o**an**ibhooss).

I want to get off at the cathedral.	**Quero descer na Sé.**	kehroo derssayr ner seh
Please let me off at the next stop.	**Por favor, quero descer na próxima paragem [parada].**	poor fervoar kehroo derssayr ner prossimmer perrahzhayng [pahrahdah]

PARAGEM [PARADA] OBRIGATÓRIA	REGULAR BUS STOP
PARAGEM [PARADA] FACULTATIVA	STOPS ON REQUEST

Boat service

Reliable ferryboats link the left bank of the Tagus river with the right. You may travel as a passenger or take your car over to Cacilhas, Barreiro or Trafaria. The ferries are very popular, and cheaper than crossing the amazing *Vinte e Cinco de Abril* bridge.

Other modes of transportation

barge	**o batelão**	oo bertehlahng[w]
bicycle	**a bicicleta**	er bissiklehter
boat	**o barco**	oo bahrkoo
motorboat	**barco a motor**	bahrkoo er mootoar
rowing-boat	**barco a remos**	bahrkoo er rehmoosh
sailing-boat	**barco à vela**	bahrkoo er vehler
funicular	**o elevador**	oo illerverdhoar
helicopter	**o helicóptero**	oo ehlikkopterroo
hitch-hiking	**à boleia [de carona]**	ah boolayer [di kahroanah]
horse-riding	**a cavalo**	ah kervahloo
hovercraft	**o aerodeslizador**	oo erehrooderzhlizzerdhoar
moped (motor-bike)	**a bicicleta a motor**	er bissiklehter er mootoar
motorcycle	**a motocicleta/ a moto**	er mottossiklehter/er mottoo
paddle-wheel steamer	**o vapor a pás**	oo verpoar er pahsh

and if you're really stuck, go...

walking	**a pé**	er peh

Around and about—Sightseeing

Here we're more concerned with the cultural aspect of life than with entertainment and, for the moment, with towns rather than the countryside. If you want a guide book, ask...

Can you recommend a good guide book on...?	Pode aconselhar-me um bom guia de...?	podher erkawngserlyahr mer oong bawng gheeer der
Is there a tourist office here?	Há um serviço de turismo por aqui?	ah oong serrveessoo der tooreeshmoo poor erkee
Where's the tourist office?	Onde fica o serviço de turismo?	awngder feeker oo serrveessoo der tooreeshmoo
What are the main points of interest?	O que há de mais interessante a visitar?	oo ker ah der mighsh eengterrerssahngter er vizzittahr
We're here for...	Estamos aqui...	ishtahmoosh erkee
only a few hours	só por algumas horas	so poor ahlgoomersh orrersh
a day	um dia	oong deeer
three days	três dias	traysh deeersh
a week	uma semana	oomer sermahner
Can you recommend a sightseeing tour?	Pode aconselhar um circuito turístico?	podher erkawngserlyahr oong sirkweetoo tooreeshtikkoo
Where does the bus start from?	De onde parte o autocarro [ônibus]?	der awngder pahrter oo owtokkahrroo [oani-bhooss]
Will it pick us up at the hotel?	Vem buscar-nos ao hotel?	vayng booshkahr noosh ow ottehl
How much does the tour cost?	Qual é o preço do circuito?	kwahl eh oo prayssoo doo sirkweetoo
What time does the tour start?	A que horas começa o circuito?	er ker orrersh koomehsser oo sirkweetoo
What bus/tram (streetcar) do we take?	Que autocarro [ônibus]/eléctrico [bonde] devemos tomar?	ker owtokkahrroo [oani-bhooss]/illehtrikkoo [bawngdi] dervehmoosh toomahr

FOR TIME OF THE DAY, see page 178

SIGHTSEEING

We'd like to rent a car for the day.	**Queríamos alugar um carro por um dia.**	kerreeermoosh erloogahr oong kahrroo poor oong deeer
Is there an English-speaking guide?	**Há aqui um guia que fale inglês?**	ah erkee oong gheeer ker fahler eengglaysh
Where is/are the...?	**Onde é/são...?**	awngder eh/sahngᵂ
abbey	**a abadia**	er erberdheeer
aquarium	**o aquário**	oo erkwahryoo
art gallery	**a galeria de arte**	er gerlerreeer der ahrter
artists' quarter	**o bairro dos artistas**	oo bighrroo doosh erteeshtersh
botanical gardens	**o jardim botânico**	oo zherrdeeng bootahngnikkoo
business district	**o centro de negócios**	oo sayngtroo der nergossyoosh
castle	**o castelo**	oo kershtehloo
cathedral	**a catedral/a Sé**	er kerterdrahl/er seh
cemetery	**o cemitério**	oo sermittehryoo
church	**a igreja**	er igrayzher
citadel	**a cidadela**	er sidahdhehler
city centre	**o centro da cidade**	oo sayngtroo der sidahdher
city walls	**as muralhas da cidade**	ersh moorahlyersh der sidahdher
concert hall	**a sala de concertos**	er sahler der kawngsayrtoosh
convent	**o convento**	oo kawngvayngtoo
convention hall	**o palácio de congressos**	oo perlahssyoo der kawnggrehssoosh
court house	**o palácio de justiça**	oo perlahssyoo der zhooshteesser
docks	**as docas**	ersh dokkersh
downtown area	**a Baixa [o centro comercial]**	er bighsher [oo sayngtroo koomerrsyahl]
exhibition	**a exposição**	er ishpoozissahngᵂ
factory	**a fábrica**	er fahbrikker
fortress	**a fortaleza**	er foorterlayzer
fountain	**a fonte**	er fawngter
gardens	**os jardins**	oosh zherrdeengsh
harbour	**o porto**	oo poartoo
lake	**o lago**	oo lahgoo
market	**o mercado**	oo merrkahdhoo
monastery	**o mosteiro**	oo mooshtayroo
monument	**o monumento**	oo moonoomayngtoo
museum	**o museu**	oo moozehoo

FOR ASKING THE WAY, see page 144

old city	a cidade antiga	er sidhahdher ahngteeger
opera house	o teatro da ópera	oo terahtroo der opperrer
palace	o palácio	oo perlahssyoo
park	o parque	oo pahrker
parliament building	o Parlamento	oo perlermayngtoo
presidential palace	o palácio presidencial	oo perlahssyoo prerziddayngsyahl
river	o rio	oo reeoo
ruins	as ruínas	ersh rweenersh
shopping centre	o centro comercial	oo sayngtroo koomerrsyahl
stadium	o estádio	oo ishtahdhyoo
statue	a estátua	er ishtahtwer
tomb	o túmulo	oo toomooloo
tower	a torre	er toarrer
university	a universidade	er oonivverrsidhahdher
windmill	o moinho de vento	oo mweenyoo der vayngtoo
zoo	o jardim zoológico	oo zherrdeeng zoo-oologgikkoo

Admission

Is... open on Sundays?	...está aberto aos domingos?	ishtah erbehrtoo owsh doomeenggoosh
When does it open/ close?	Quando abre/ fecha?	kwahngdoo ahbrer/ fehsher
How much is the entrance fee?	Quanto custa o bilhete de entrada [a entrada]?	kwahngtoo kooshter oo billyayter der ayngtrahdher [ah ayngtrahdhah]
Is there any reduction for students/ children?	Fazem desconto a estudantes/ crianças?	fahzayng dershkawngtoo er ishtoodhahngtersh/ kryahngssersh
Have you a guide book (in English)?	Tem um guia (em inglês)?	tayng oong gheeer (ayng eengglaysh)
Can I buy a catalogue?	Posso comprar um catálogo?	possoo kawngprahr oong kertahloogoo
Is it all right to take pictures?	É permitido tirar fotografias?	eh perrmitteedhoo tirrahr footoogrerfeeersh

ENTRADA LIVRE	ADMISSION FREE
PROIBIDO TIRAR FOTOGRAFIAS	NO CAMERAS ALLOWED

Who—What—When?

What's that building?	**O que é aquele edifício?**	oo ker eh erkayler idhiffeessyoo
Who was the...?	**Quem foi o...?**	kayng fawng^y oo
architect	**arquitecto**	errkittehtoo
artist	**artista**	errteeshter
painter	**pintor**	peengtoar
sculptor	**escultor**	ishkooltoar
Who painted that picture?	**Quem pintou aquele quadro?**	kayng peengtoa erkayler kwahdroo
When did he live?	**Em que época viveu?**	ayng ker ehpokker vivvehoo
When was it built?	**Quando foi construído?**	kwahngdoo fawng^y kawngshtrweedhoo
Where's the house where... lived?	**Onde fica a casa em que viveu...?**	awngder feeker er kahzer ayng ker vivvehoo
We're interested in...	**Estamos interessados em...**	ishtahmoosh eengterrerssahdhoosh ayng
antiques	**antiguidades**	ahngtigweedhahdhersh
archaeology	**arqueologia**	erkyooloozheeer
art	**arte**	ahrter
botany	**botânica**	bootahngnikker
ceramics	**cerâmica**	sehrahngmikker
coins	**moedas**	mwehdhersh
crafts	**artesanato**	errterzernahtoo
fine arts	**belas artes**	behlersh ahrtersh
folk arts	**arte popular**	ahrter poopoolahr
furniture	**mobiliário [mobília]**	moobhillyahryoo [moabheelyah]
geology	**geologia**	zherooloozheeer
history	**história**	ishtorryer
medicine	**medicina**	merdhisseener
music	**música**	moozikker
natural history	**ciências naturais**	syayngsyersh nertoorighsh
ornithology	**ornitologia**	ornitooloozheeer
painting	**pintura**	peengtoorer
pottery	**olaria**	ollerreeer
prehistory	**pré-história**	preh-ishtorryer
sculpture	**escultura**	ishkooltoorer
zoology	**zoologia**	zoo-ooloozheeer
Where's the... department?	**Onde fica o departamento de...?**	awngder feeker oo derperrtermayngtoo der

Just the adjective you've been looking for...

It's...	É...	eh
amazing	espantoso	ishpahng**toa**zoo
awful	horroroso	oorroo**roa**zoo
beautiful	lindo	**leeng**doo
gloomy	lúgubre	**loo**goobrer
impressive	grandioso	grahng**dyoa**zoo
interesting	interessante	eengterrers**sahng**ter
magnificent	magnífico	mah**gnee**fikkoo
monumental	monumental	moonoomayng**tahl**
strange	estranho	ish**trah**nyoo
superb	estupendo	ishtoo**payng**doo
terrible	terrível	terr**ree**vehl
terrifying	pavoroso	pervoo**roa**zoo
tremendous	tremendo	trer**mayng**doo
ugly	feio	**fay**oo
weird	fantástico	fahng**tahsh**tikkoo

Religious services

Portugal, predominantly Roman Catholic, is rich in cathedrals and churches worth visiting. Fátima—probably the most famous pilgrimage centre in the Iberian peninsula—is about 130 km north-east of Lisbon.

Is there a/an... near here?	Há uma... aqui perto?	ah **oo**mer...er**kee** pehr**too**
Catholic/Protestant church	igreja católica/ protestante	i**gray**zher ker**tol**likker/ prootersh**tahng**ter
synagogue	sinagoga	siner**gog**ger
mosque	mesquita	mersh**kee**ter
At what time is...?	A que horas é...?	er ker **orr**ersh eh
mass/the service	a missa/o ofício [serviço religioso]	er **mee**sser/oo oo**fee**ssyoo [sehr**vee**ssoa rehli**zhoa**zoa]
Where can I find a... who speaks English?	Onde posso encontrar um... que fale inglês?	**awng**der **poss**oo ayng**kawng**trahr oong... ker **fah**ler eeng**glaysh**
priest/minister	padre/sacerdote [pastor]	**pah**drer/sersserr**dot**ter [pahs**toar**]
rabbi	rabino	rer**bhee**noo

Relaxing

Cinema (movies)—Theatre

In Portugal, films are usually shown in their original language, with Portuguese subtitles. Separate performances are the rule, beginning about 3 p.m., with the last show of the night at around 9.30 p.m. In Brazil showings are normally continuous, without intermissions, starting at 2 p.m.

In Portuguese theatres there are matinées and two evening performances on Sundays. Musical reviews (*revistas*—rer**veesh**tersh) are very popular.

You can find out what's playing from the newspapers and billboards or from magazines like "This Week in…"

Have you a copy of "This Week in Lisbon"?	**Tem um número de "This Week in Lisbon"?**	tayng oong **noo**merroo der "this week in Lisbon"
What's showing at the cinema tonight?	**O que vai [passa] no cinema esta noite?**	oo ker vigh [**pah**ssah] noo **sin**nehmer **ehsh**ter **nawng**Yter
What's playing at the… Theatre?	**O que vai [passa] no Teatro…?**	oo ker vigh [**pah**ssah] noo te**rah**troo
What sort of play is it?	**Que género de peça é?**	ker **zheh**nerroo der **peh**sser eh
Who is it by?	**Quem é o autor?**	kayng eh oo ow**toar**
Can you recommend (a)…?	**Pode aconselhar- -me…?**	podher erkawngser**lyahr** mer
good film	**um bom filme**	oong bawng **feel**mer
comedy	**uma comédia**	**oo**mer koo**meh**dhyer
something light	**algo de divertido**	**ahl**goo der divverr**teed**hoo
musical	**uma comédia musical**	**oo**mer koo**meh**dhyer mooz**ikk**ahl
revue	**uma revista**	**oo**mer rer**veesh**ter
thriller	**um filme policial**	oong **feel**mer poolis**syahl**
western	**um filme de cow- -boys**	oong **feel**mer der "cow boys"

At what theatre is that new play by... being performed?	**Em que teatro está [passa] a nova peça de...?**	ayng ker terahtroo ishtah [pahssah] er novver pehsser der
Where's that new film by... being shown?	**Onde vai [passa] o novo filme de...?**	awngder vigh [pahssah] oo noavoo feelmer der
Who's in it?	**Quem são os actores?**	kayng sahng^w oosh ahtoarersh
Who's the director?	**Quem é o realizador?**	kayng eh oo ryerlizzer**dhoar**
What time does it begin?	**A que horas começa o espectáculo?**	er ker orrersh koomehsser oo ishpehtahkooloo
What time does the show end?	**A que horas termina o espectáculo?**	er ker orrersh terrmeener oo ishpehtahkooloo
What time does the first evening showing start?	**A que horas começa a primeira sessão da noite?**	er ker orrersh koomehsser er primmayrer serssahng^w der nawng^{y}ter
Are there any tickets for tonight?	**Ainda há bilhetes [entradas] para esta noite?**	ereengder ah billyaytersh [ayngtrahdhahss] perrer ehshter nawng^{y}ter
How much are the tickets?	**Quanto custa cada bilhete?***	kwahngtoo kooshter kerdher billyayter
I want to reserve 2 tickets for the show on Friday evening.	**Queria reservar 2 bilhetes [entradas] para o espectáculo de sexta-feira à noite?**	kerreeer rerzerrvahr 2 billyaytersh [ayngtrahdhahss] perrer oo ishpehtahkooloo der sayshter fayrer ah nawng^{y}ter
Can I have a ticket for the matinée on Tuesday?	**Queria um bilhete* para a matinée de terça-feira.**	kerreeer oong billyayter perrer er mahtinnay der tayrser fayrer
I want a seat in the stalls (orchestra).	**Quero um bilhete* de plateia.**	kehroo oong billyayter der plahtehyer
Not too far back.	**Não muito atrás.**	nahng^w moong^{y}too ertrash
Somewhere in the middle.	**Ao meio.**	ow mayoo
How much are the seats in the circle (mezzanine)?	**Quanto custam os bilhetes [as entradas] de balcão?**	kwahngtoo kooshtahng oosh billyaytersh [ahss ayngtrahdhahss] der bahl**kawng^w**

* In Brazil: **entrada** (ayng**trah**dhah).

| May I please have a programme? | **Pode dar-me um programa, por favor?** | podher dahr mer oong proogrermer poor fervoar |
| Can I check this coat? | **Pode guardar-me este casaco?** | podher gwerrdahr mer ayshter kerzahkoo |

Lamento, está esgotado.	I'm sorry, we're sold out.
Temos apenas alguns lugares na plateia/no balcão.	There are only a few seats left in the stalls (orchestra)/circle (balcony).
Só há lugares em pé.	There's standing room only.
O bilhete, por favor.	May I see your ticket?
Este/Aquele é o seu lugar.	This is your seat.

RELAXING

Opera—Ballet—Concert

A music and ballet festival, featuring international artists, takes place every year (in May—June) at the Gulbenkian Centre for Arts and Culture in Lisbon. There's also a yearly opera season.

Where's the opera house?	**Onde fica o teatro da ópera?**	awngder feeker oo terahtroo der opperrer
Where's the concert hall?	**Onde fica a sala de concertos?**	awngder feeker er sahler der kawngsayrtoosh
What's on at the opera tonight?	**Que ópera se representa esta noite?**	ker opperrer ser rerprerzayngter ehshter nawngᵛter
Who's singing?	**Quem canta?**	kayng kahngter
Who's dancing?	**Quem dança?**	kayng dahngser
What time does the programme start?	**A que horas começa o espectáculo?**	er ker orrersh koomehsser oo ishpehtahkooloo
What orchestra is playing?	**Que orquestra toca [está tocando]?**	ker oorkehshtrer tokker [istah toakahngdoa]
What are they playing?	**O que tocam?**	oo ker tokkahng
Who's the conductor?	**Quem é o maestro?**	kayng eh oo merehshtroo

FOR TIPPING, see page 1

Fado—Night-clubs

In major cities you can dance in most of the de luxe and first class hotels. Conventional night-clubs and discotheques, in consequence, are few. Be sure to wear a dark suit and a tie.

Far more interesting are the *casas de fado* or *adegas típicas,* little, late-night restaurants where you eat and drink while listening to the *fado.* The best spots in Lisbon are located in the *Alfama* and *Bairro Alto* districts. *Fado,* a type of song native to Lisbon, expresses deep feelings of melancholy and *saudade* ("regret of absence"). Accompanied by two or three guitars and a viol, the *fadista,* all in black, sings in a hushed room—even at the end of the song the audience isn't supposed to applaud. There are two kinds of *fado*—the traditional *fado* of Lisbon, and the Coimbra *fado,* adapted to more modern and regional tastes.

Can you recommend a good night-club?	**Pode indicar-me um bom nightclub [uma boa buate]?**	podher eengdikkahr mer oong bawng "nightclub" [oomah boaah bwahti]
Is there a floor show?	**Há variedades [show]?**	ah verryerdahdhersh ["show"]
What time does the floor show start?	**A que horas começa o espectáculo [show]?**	er ker orrersh koomehsser oo ishpehtahkooloo ["show"]
Is evening dress necessary?	**É necessário trajo [traje] de noite?**	eh nersserssahryoo trahzhoo [trahzhi] der nawngᵛter

And once inside...

A table for 2, please.	**Uma mesa para 2, por favor.**	oomer mayzer perrer 2 poor fervoar
My name's... I reserved a table for 4.	**Chamo-me... E reservei uma mesa para 4 pessoas.**	shahmoo mer...ee rerzerrvay oomer mayzer perrer 4 perssoaersh
We haven't got a reservation.	**Não reservámos.**	nahngʷ rerzerrvahmoosh

Dancing

Where can we go dancing?	**Onde podemos ir dançar?**	awngder poodhaymoosh eer dahngsahr
Is there a discotheque in town?	**Há alguma buate na cidade?**	ah algoomer bwahter ner sidhahdher
There's a dance at the...	**Há um baile em...**	ah oong bighler ayng
Would you like to dance?	**Quer dançar?**	kehr dahngsahr
May I have this dance?	**Concede-me esta dança?**	kawngsehdher mer ehshter dahngser

Do you happen to play...?

On a rainy day, this page may solve your problems.

Do you happen to play chess?	**Joga xadrez?**	zhogger sherdraysh
I'm afraid I don't.	**Lamento, mas não jogo.**	lermayngtoo mersh nawng zhoggoo
No, but I'll give you a game of draughts (checkers).	**Não, mas posso jogar às damas.**	nawng mersh possoo zhoggahr ersh dahmersh
king	**o rei**	oo ray
queen	**a rainha**	er rereenyer
castle (rook)	**o castelo [a torre]**	oo kershtehloo [ah toarri]
bishop	**o bispo**	oo beeshpoo
knight	**o cavalo**	oo kervahloo
pawn	**o peão**	oo perahng^w
Check!	**Cheque!**	shehker
Checkmate!	**Chequemate!**	shehkermahter
Do you play cards?	**Joga às cartas?**	zhogger ersh kahrtersh
bridge	**bridge**	breedzher
canasta	**canasta**	kernahshter
whist	**whist**	whist
pontoon (21)	**pontão**	pawngtahng^w
poker	**poker**	pokkehr

RELAXING

ace	o ás	oo ahsh
king	o rei	oo ray
queen	a rainha	er rereenyer
jack	o valete	oo verlehter
joker	o diabo [o coringa]	oo deeahboo [oo koareenggah]
hearts	as copas	ersh koppersh
diamonds	os ouros	oosh oaroosh
clubs	os paus	oosh powsh
spades	as espadas	ersh ishpahdersh

Casino

Estoril, a well-known luxury summer resort about 13 miles west of Lisbon, has a casino where you can gamble all year round. Other casinos in Figueira da Foz, Póvoa de Varzim and Espinho are open from June to November. There are also casinos at Alvor, Vilamoura and Monte Gordo in the fashionable province of Algarve in southern Portugal.

Bullfight

The Portuguese version of the bullfight (*corrida à Portuguesa* or *tourada*) is quite different from the Spanish *corrida*. In Spain, the fashion has always been to fight the bull on foot whereas in Portugal the characteristic style is on horseback.

Moreover, killing the bull is forbidden in Portugal since the 18th century. Therefore, the bullfight emphasizes the elegance, daring and skill of the horseman *(cavaleiro)* and his thoroughbred.

When the trumpet sounds, the *cavaleiro* on horseback and the bull enter the ring. While the bull charges, his horns covered with leather bandages *(embeladas)*, the horse sidesteps allowing the *cavaleiro* to thrust a shaft *(ferro)* in the bull's shoulder. The *cavaleiro* goes on goading the beast. When the bull shows signs of exhaustion, the *cavaleiro*

RELAXING

makes way for the *moços de forcado,* a team of eight strong men led by a tackler *(pegador)*. When the bull charges, the tackler tries to hold the beast to a standstill with his fellow's help.

There are three authorized ways of tackling the bull: face to face *(de cara)*, back to front *(de costas)*, and sideways on *(de cernelha)*. This somewhat rodeo-like performance is the most exciting part of the spectacle and earns great applause from the audience.

The best (and most expensive) seats are located in the shade *(sombra)* and in the front rows *(barreira)*. Next come the *sol e sombra* (sun and shade) seats. Think it over before you choose the cheaper category, *sol* (sun): the sun can be too much for most visitors.

Bullfighting takes place—from Easter to October—almost every Sunday afternoon in many places, and frequently on Thursday evenings in Lisbon (at *Campo Pequeno*).

| I'd like to see a bullfight. | **Queria ver uma tourada.** | kerreeer vayr oomer toarahdher |
| I want a seat in the shade/in the sun. | **Queria um lugar à sombra/ao sol.** | kerreeer oong loogahr ao sawngbrer/ow sol |

Other sports

The Portuguese are football (soccer) fans. Remember that one of the world's most famous teams, *Benfica,* is based in Lisbon.

Golf, tennis, fishing and diving are also very popular. A good place to go to enjoy these sports is the province of Algarve, where three wonderful golf courses await the amateur, as well as a number of riding schools.

And if you're fond of sailing, go to Cascais or Estoril. You'll probably be lucky enough to attend one of the many regattas which take place throughout the year.

Is there a football (soccer) match anywhere today?	**Há algum desafio [alguma partida] de futebol hoje em qualquer parte?**	ah ahl**goong** derzer**fee**oo [ahl**goo**mah pahr**tee**dhah] der footer**bol** oazher ayng kwahl**kehr** pahrter
I'd like to see a boxing match.	**Gostaria de ver um combate de boxe.**	goosh**terree**er der vayr oong kawng**bah**ter der boks
Who's playing?	**Quem joga?**	kayng **zho**gger
Can you get me 2 tickets?	**Pode arranjar-me 2 bilhetes [entradas]?**	**po**dher errrahng**zhahr** mer 2 bill**yay**tersh [ayng**trah**dhahs]
Where's the nearest golf course?	**Onde fica o campo de golf mais próximo?**	awng**der fee**ker oo **kahng**poo der golf mighsh **pross**immoo
Can we hire (rent) clubs?	**Podemos alugar clubes?**	poo**dhay**moosh erloo**gahr kloo**bhersh
Where are the tennis courts?	**Onde ficam os campos de ténis?**	awng**der fee**kahng^w oosh **kahng**poosh der **teh**nis
Can I hire rackets?	**Posso alugar raquetas?**	**poss**oo erloo**gahr** rer**kay**tersh
What's the charge per...?	**Qual é o preço por...?**	kwahl eh oo **pray**ssoo poor
day/round/hour	**dia/jogo/hora**	**dee**er/**zhoa**goo/**or**rer
Where's the nearest race course (track)?	**Onde o hipódromo mais próximo?**	awng**der fee**ker oo ip**po**droomoo mighsh **pross**immoo
What's the admission charge?	**Qual é o preço de entrada?**	kwahl eh oo **pray**ssoo der ayng**trah**dher
Is there a swimming pool near here?	**Há alguma piscina aqui perto?**	ah ahl**goo**mer pis**see**ner er**kee peh**rtoo
Is it open-air/ indoors/heated?	**É ao ar livre/coberta/aquecida?**	eh ow ahr **lee**vrer/koo**bheh**rter/erkeh**see**dher
Can one swim in the lake/river?	**Pode-se nadar no lago/rio?**	**po**dher ser ner**dhahr** noo **lah**goo/**ree**oo
Is there any good fishing around here?	**Há algum bom lugar para pescar aqui perto?**	ah ahl**goong** bawng loo**gahr** perrer persh**kahr** er**kee peh**rtoo
Do I need a permit?	**É preciso uma licença de pesca?**	eh prer**ssee**zoo **oo**mer lis**sayng**ser der **pehsh**ker

On the beach

Is it safe for swimming?	**Pode-se nadar sem perigo?**	podher ser nerd**h**ahr sayng perreegoo
Is there a lifeguard?	**Há um banheiro [salva-vidas]?**	ah oong bern**y**ayroo [**sah**lvah **veed**hahss]
Is it safe for children?	**Não há perigo para as crianças?**	nahng**w** ah perreegoo perrer ersh kr**y**ahngsersh
The sea is very calm.	**O mar é muito calmo.**	oo mahr eh **moong**v̇too **kah**lmoo
There are some big waves.	**Há ondas grandes.**	ah **awng**dersh grahng- dersh
Are there any dangerous currents?	**Há correntes perigosas?**	ah koorrayngtersh perrig**go**zzersh
What time is high/ low tide?	**A que horas é a maré alta/baixa?**	er ker orrersh eh er **merreh** ahlter/**bigh**sher
What's the temperature of the water?	**Qual é a temperatura da água?**	kwahl eh er tayngperrer- **toor**er der **ah**gwer
I want to hire a/an...	**Queria alugar...**	kerr**eee**r erloo**gah**r
air mattress	**um colchão pneumático**	oong koolshahng**w** pnehoo**mah**tikkoo
bathing hut	**uma barraca**	oomer berr**rah**ker
deck chair	**uma cadeira de encosto**	oomer kerd**hay**rer der ayng**koash**too
skin-diving equipment	**o equipamento de mergulhador**	oo erkipper**mayng**too der merrgoolyerd**hoar**
sunshade	**um guarda-sol**	oong **gwahr**der sol
surfboard*	**uma prancha**	oomer prahng**sher**
some water skis	**skis [esquis] aquáticos**	skeesh [ehs**kiss**[erkw**ah**tikkoosh
Where can I rent a...?	**Onde posso alugar...?**	**awng**der posso erloo**gah**r
canoe	**uma canoa**	oomer kern**oa**er
motor boat	**um barco a motor**	oong **bahr**koo er moo**toar**
rowing-boat	**um barco a remos**	oong **bahr**koo er **reh**moosh
sailing-boat	**um barco à vela**	oong **bahr**koo ah **veh**ler
What's the charge per hour?	**Qual é o preço por hora?**	kwahl eh oo **prays**soo poor **or**rer

* In Portugal, surfing is prohibited on public beaches.

| **PROIBIDO TOMAR BANHO** | **PRAIA PRIVADA** |
| NO BATHING | PRIVATE BEACH |

Beach Sports

Here are some ideas for a long day on the beach:

badminton rackets	**umas raquetas de badminton**	oomersh rahkehtersh der bahdmeenggton
beach ball	**uma bola de praia**	oomer boller der prigher
breathing pipe (snorkel tube)	**um tubo de respi- ração para pesca submarina**	oong toobhoo der rershpi- rrerssahng^w perrer pehshker soobmerreener
flippers (swimming fins)	**umas barbatanas**	oomersh berbertahnersh
goggles	**uns óculos de pro- tecção**	oongsh okkooloosh der prootehssahng^w
inflatable boat	**um barco pneu- mático**	oong bahrkoo pnehoo- mahtikkoo
kite	**um papagaio**	oong perpergighoo
swimming belt	**uma bóia**	oomer boyer
table-tennis paddles	**umas raquetas de pingpong**	oomersh rahkehtersh der "pingpong"

RELAXING

90

Camping—Countryside

CAMPING – COUNTRYSIDE

Campers in Portugal need an International Camping Card, obtainable from camping clubs or from one of the motoring associations.

Mostly located in or near coastal resorts, the Portuguese camping sites offer very reasonable prices and amenities.

For a complete list of all the campsites in Brazil, with local maps and details of facilities and travel connections, consult the annual camping guide *(Guia de Camping)* sold at most news-stands.

Can we camp here?	**Podemos acampar aqui?**	poodhehmoosh erkahng-pahr erkee
Where can one camp for the night?	**Onde se poderá acampar por esta noite?**	awngder ser poodherrah erkahngpahr poor ehshter nawng^vter
Is there a camping site near here?	**Há algum parque de campismo [acampamento] por aqui perto?**	ah ahlgoong pahrker der kahngpeeshmoo [ah-kahngpahmayngtoa] poor erkee pehrtoo
May we camp in your field?	**Podemos acampar no seu terreno?**	poodhehmoosh erkahng-pahr noo sehoo terr-rehnoo
Can we park our car-avan (trailer) here?	**Podemos deixar a nossa roulotte aqui?**	poodhehmoosh dayshahr er nosser roolotter erkee
May we light a fire?	**Podemos acender uma fogueira?**	poodhehmoosh erssayng-dayr oomer foogayrer
Is drinking water available?	**Tem água potável?**	tayng ahgwer pootahvehl
Are there shopping facilities on the site?	**Há possibilidade de se fazer compras no campo?**	ah poossibhillidhahdher der ser ferzayr kawngprersh noo kahngpoo
Are there...?	**Há...?**	ah
baths	**banhos**	bernyoosh
showers	**chuveiros**	shoovayroosh
toilets	**retretes**	rertrehtersh

What's the charge...?	**Qual é o custo...?**	kwahl eh oo **koosh**too
per day	**por dia**	poor **dee**er
per person	**por pessoa**	poor pe**ssoa**er
for a car	**por um carro**	poor oong **kahr**roo
for a tent	**por uma tenda**	poor **oo**mer **tayng**der
for a caravan (trailer)	**por roulotte**	poor **roo**lotter

| Is there a youth hostel near here? | **Há algum albergue de juventude aqui perto?** | ah ah**goong** ahl**behr**ger der zhoovayng**too**dher er**kee** **pehr**too |

| Do you know anyone who can put us up for the night? | **Conhece alguém que nos possa albergar por uma noite?** | koony**ehss**er ahl**gayng** ker noosh **poss**er ahl**berr**gahr poor **oo**mer **nawng**yter |

PROIBIDO ACAMPAR	**PROIBIDO A ROULOTTES**
NO CAMPING	NO CARAVANS (TRAILERS)

Landmarks

barn	**o celeiro**	oo ser**lay**roo
beach	**a praia**	er **prigh**er
bridge	**a ponte**	er **pawng**ter
brook	**o ribeiro [riacho]**	oo rib**bhay**roo [**ryah**shoa]
canal	**o canal**	oo ker**nahl**
castle	**o castelo**	oo kersh**teh**loo
church	**a igreja**	er i**gray**zher
cliff	**o penhasco**	oo pern**yahsh**koo
copse	**a mata**	er **mah**ter
crossroads	**a encruzilhada [o cruzamento]**	er ayngkroozill**yah**dher [oa kroozah**mayng**toa]
farm	**a quinta [fazenda]**	er **keeng**ter [fah**zayng**dah]
field	**o campo**	oo **kahng**poo
footpath	**o caminho**	oo ker**mee**nyoo
forest	**a floresta**	er floo**rehsh**ter
fortress	**a fortaleza**	er foarter**lay**zer
hamlet	**o lugarejo**	oo looger**ray**zhoo
heath	**a charneca [o urze]**	er sherr**neh**ker [oo **oor**zi]
highway	**a auto-estrada**	er **ow**too ish**trah**dher
hill	**a colina**	er koo**lee**ner
house	**a casa**	er **kah**zer
hut	**a barraca**	er berr**rah**ker

inn	o albergue	oo ahlbehrger
lake	o lago	oo lahgoo
marsh	o pântano/o paúl	oo pahngternoo/oo perool
moorland	a charneca	er sherrnehker
mountain	a serra	er sehrrer
mountain range	a cordilheira	er koordillyayrer
path	o caminho	oo kermeenyoo
peak	o pico/o cume	oo peekoo/oo koomer
pool	a poça	er poasser
railway track	a linha férrea [estrada de ferro]	er leenyer fehrryer [istrahdah dee fehrroa]
river	o rio	oo reeoo
road	a estrada	er ishtrahdher
ruins	as ruínas	ersh rweenersh
sea	o mar	oo mahr
spring	a nascente	er nerssayngter
stream	o rio	oo reeoo
swamp	o lodaçal	oo loodherssahl
tower	a torre	er toarrer
track	a pista	er peeshter
tree	a árvore	er ahrvoorer
valley	o vale	oo vahler
village	a aldeia	er ahldayer
vineyard	a vinha	er veenyer
waterfall	a queda de água	er kehdher der ahgwer
well	o poço	oo poassoo
windmill	o moinho de vento	oo mweenyoo der vayngtoo
wood	o bosque	oo boshker

PROIBIDA A ENTRADA
NO TRESPASSING

| What's the name of that river? | Como se chama este rio? | koamoo ser shahmer ayshter reeoo |
| How high is that mountain? | Que altitude tem aquela montanha? | ker ahltittoodher tayng erkehler mawngternyer |

And if you're tired of walking, you can always try hitchhiking, though you may have to wait a long time for a lift.

| Can you give me a lift to...? | Pode dar-me uma boleia [carona] para...? | podher dahr mer oomer boolayer [kahroanah] perrer |

Making friends

Introductions

Here are a few phrases to get you started:

How do you do?	**Muito prazer.**	moong^vtoo prerzayr
How are you?	**Como está?**	koamoo ishtah
Very well, thank you.	**Bem, obrigado/a.**	bayng oobriggahdhoo/er
May I introduce Miss Philips?	**Posso apresentar--lhe a Menina [senhorita] Philips?**	possoo erprerzayngtahr lyer er merneener [saynyoareetah] philips
I'd like you to meet a friend of mine.	**Quero apresentar--lhe um amigo/ uma amiga.**	kehroo erprerzayngtahr lyer oong ermeegoo/oomer ermeeger
John, this is...	**João, apresento--lhe...**	zhooahng^w erprerzayngtoo lyer
My name's...	**Chamo-me...**	shahmoo mer
Glad to know you.	**Muito prazer em conhecê-lo/la.**	moong^vtoo prerzayr ayng koonyer**ssay** loo/ler

Follow-up

How long have you been here?	**Há quanto tempo está cá*?**	ah **kwang**too **tayng**poo ishtah kah
We've been here a week.	**Estamos cá* há uma semana.**	ishtah**moosh** kah eh **oo**mer sermahner
Is this your first visit?	**É a primeira vez que cá* vem?**	eh er prim**may**rer vayz ker kah vayng
No, we came here last year.	**Não, já cá* viémos o ano passado.**	nahng^w zhah kah vyeh**moosh** oo **er**noo persssahdhoo
Are you enjoying your stay?	**Está a gostar [gostando] da estadia?**	ishtah er goosh**tahr** [go-**stahng**doa] der ishter-**dheeer**
Yes, I like... very much.	**Sim, gosto muito...**	seeng **gosh**too **moong**^vtoo
Are you on your own?	**Está sòzinho/a?**	ishtah sozzeenyoo/nyer

* In Brazil: **aqui** (erkee).

I'm with...	Estou com...	ishtoa kawng
my husband	o meu marido	oo mehoo merreedhoo
my wife	a minha mulher	er meenyer moolyehr
my family	a minha família	er meenyer fermeelyer
my parents	os meus pais	oosh mehoosh pighsh
some friends	uns amigos	oongsh ermeegoosh
Where do you come from?	De onde vem?	der awngder vayng
What part of... do you come from?	De que parte de... vem?	der ker pahrter der... vayng
I'm from...	Venho de...	vehnyoo der
Where are you staying?	Onde está hospedado?	awngder ishtah oashperdhahdhoo
I'm a student	Sou estudante.	soa ishtoodhangter
We're here on holiday.	Estamos aqui de férias.	ishtahmoosh erkee der fehryersh
I'm here on business.	Estou aqui em [à] negócios.	ishtoa erkee ayng [ah] nergossyoosh
We hope to see you again soon.	Esperamos vê-lo de novo dentro em breve.	ishperrahmoosh vay loo der noavoo dayngtroo ayng brehver
See you later/See you tomorrow.	Até logo/Até amanhã.	erteh loggoo/erteh ahmernyahng

The weather

Always a good topic for conversation, in Portugal as much as elsewhere. So...

What a lovely day!	Que lindo dia!	ker leengdoo deeer
What awful weather!	Que mau tempo!	ker mow tayngpoo
Isn't it cold/hot today?	Que frio/calor está hoje!	ker freeoo/kerloar ishtah oazher
Do you think it'll ...tomorrow?	Pensa que... amanhã?	payngser ker... ahmernyahng
rain/snow	chove/neva	shovver/nehver
clear up/be sunny	o tempo melhora/ haverá sol	oo tayngpoo merlyorrer/ erverrah sol

Invitations

My wife and I would like you to dine with us on…	**A minha mulher e eu queríamos convidá-lo para jantar…**	er meenyer moolyehr ee ehoo kerreeeermoosh kawngviddah loo perrer zhahngtahr
Can you come to dinner tomorrow night?	**Pode vir jantar amanhã à noite?**	podher veer zhahngtahr ahmernyahng ah nawngᵛter
Can you join us for a drink this evening?	**Venha beber qualquer coisa connosco, esta tarde.**	vernyer berbhayr kwahlkehr kawngᵛzer kawngnoashkoo ehshter tahrder
There's a party. Are you coming?	**Há uma festa. Pode vir?**	ah oomer fehshter. podher veer
That's very kind of you.	**É muito amável da sua parte.**	eh moongᵛtoo ermahvehl der sooer pahrter
Great. I'd love to come.	**Óptimo. Virei com muito gosto [prazer].**	ottimmoo. virray kawng moongᵛtoo goashtoo [prahzayr]
What time shall we come?	**A que horas devemos vir?**	er ker orresh dervehmoosh veer
May I bring a friend?	**Posso trazer um amigo/uma amiga?**	possoo trerzayr oong ermeegoo/oomer ermeeger
I'm afraid we've got to go now.	**Lamento, mas temos de partir.**	lermæyngtoo mersh taymoosh der perrteer
Next time you must come to visit us.	**Para a próxima vez, terá de vir a nossa casa.**	perrer er prossimmer vayzh terrah der veer er nosser kahzer
Thanks for the evening. It was great.	**Obrigado/a pela festa. Foi estupenda.**	oobriggahdhoo/er perler fehshter. fawngᵛ ishtoopayngder

Dating

Would you like a cigarette?	**Posso oferecer-lhe um cigarro?**	possoo ooferrerssayr lyer oong siggahrroo
Do you have a light, please?	**Tem lume [fósforos], por favor?**	tayng loomer [fosforroass] poor fervoar
Can I get you a drink?	**Que quer beber?**	ker kehr berbhayr

Are your waiting for someone?	Espera alguém?	ishpehrer ahlgayng
Are you free this evening?	Está livre esta noite?	ishtah leevrer ehshter nawngᵛter
Would you like to go out with me tonight?	Posso convidá-la a sair comigo esta noite?	possoo kawngvidhah ler er sereer koomeegoo ehshter nawngᵛter
Would you like to go dancing?	Gostaria de ir dançar?	gooshterreeer der eer dahngsahr
I know a good disco-theque/restaurant.	Conheço uma boa buate/um bom restaurante.	koonyayssoo oomer boaer bwahter/oong bawng rershtowrahngter
Shall we go to the cinema (movies)?	Vamos ao cinema?	vahmoosh ow sinnehmer
Would you like to go for a drive?	Vamos dar um passeio de carro?	vahmoosh dahr oong perssayoo der kahrroo
I'd love to, thank you.	Com muito gosto [prazer].	kawng moongᵛtoo goashtoo [prahzayr]
Where shall we meet?	Onde nos encontramos?	awngder noosh ayngkawngtrahmoosh
I'll pick you up at your hotel.	Vou buscá-la ao seu hotel.	voa booshkah ler ow sehoo ottehl
I'll call for you at 8.	Passo a buscá-la às 8.	pahssoo er booshkah ler ersh 8
May I take you home?	Posso acompanhá-la a casa?	possoo erkawngpernyah ler er kahzer
Can I see you again tomorrow?	Posso vê-la amanhã?	possoo vay ler ahmernyahng
Thank you, it's been a wonderful evening.	Obrigado por esta noite tão agradável.	oobriggahdhoo poor eshter nawngᵛter tahngʷ ergrerdahvehl
What's your telephone number?	Qual é o seu número de telefone?	kwahl eh oo sehoo noomerroo der terlerfonner
Do you live alone?	Vive só?	veever soh
What time is your last bus?	A que horas parte o seu último autocarro [ônibus]?	er ker orrersh pahrter oo sehoo ooltimmoo owtookahrroo [oanibhooss]

Shopping guide

This shopping guide is designed to help you find what you want with ease, accuracy and speed. It features:

1. A list of all major shops, stores and services (p. 98).
2. Some general expressions required when shopping to allow you to be specific and selective (p. 100).
3. Full details of the shops and services most likely to concern you. Here you'll find advice, alphabetical lists of items and conversion charts listed under the headings below.

		Page
Bookshop	books, magazines, newspapers, stationery	104
Camping	camping equipment	106
Chemist's (drugstore)	medicine, first-aid, cosmetics, toilet articles	108
Clothing	clothes, shoes, accessories	112
Electrical appliances	radios, tape-recorders, shavers, records	119
Hairdresser's	barber's, ladies' hairdresser's, beauty salon	121
Jeweller's	jewellery, watches, watch repairs	123
Laundry– Dry cleaning	usual facilities	126
Photography	cameras, accessories, films, developing	127
Provisions	this is confined to basic items required for picnics	130
Souvenirs	souvenirs, gifts, fancy goods	132
Tobacconist's	smoker's supplies	133

SHOPPING GUIDE

Shops, stores and services

In Portugal, you can buy bread and milk as early as 7.30 a.m., but most shops are open from about 9 a.m. to 7 p.m., with a lunch break from 1 to 3 p.m. All shops close on Sundays, national holidays and sometimes on local festival days. A very few remain open on Saturday afternoon. Brazilian stores are open from 8 or 9 a.m. to 6 p.m. or even later. Some local food stores open on Sunday mornings.

Where's the nearest...?	Onde fica...mais próximo/próxima?	awngder feeker...mighsh prossimmoo/prossimmer
antique shop	o antiquário	oo ahngtikwahryoo
art gallery	a galeria de arte	er gerlerreeer der ahrter
baker's	a padaria	er pahdherreeer
bank	o banco	oo bahngkoo
barber	o barbeiro	oo berrbayroo
beauty salon	o instituto de beleza	oo eengshtittootoo der berlayzer
bookshop	a livraria	er livrerreeer
butcher's	o talho [açougue]	oo tahlyoo [ahssoagee]
camera store	o fotógrafo*	oo footogrerfoo
candy store	a confeitaria	er kawngfayterreeer
chemist's	a farmácia	er ferrmahssyer
cobbler	o sapateiro	oo serpertayroo
confectioner's	a pastelaria [confeitaria]	er pershterlerreeer [kawngfaytahreeah]
dairy	a leitaria	er layterreeer
delicatessen	a salsicharia [delicatess]	er sahlsisherreeer [daylikkahtehss]
dentist	o dentista	oo dayngteeshter
department store	o armazém [empório]	oo errmerzahngv [ayngporryoa]
doctor	o médico	oo mehdhikkoo
draper's	a loja de tecidos	er lozher der tersseedhoosh
dressmaker's	a costureira	er kooshtoorayrer
drugstore	a farmácia	er ferrmahssyer
dry cleaner's	a lavandaria a seco	er lervahngderreeer er saykoo
dry goods store	a retrosaria	er rertroozerreeer

* In Brazil: **loja de artigos fotográficos** (lozhah dee ahrteegoass foatoagrah-fikkoass).

fishmonger's	a peixaria	er paysherreeer
greengrocer's	o hortaliceiro [a quitanda]	oo orterlissayroo [ah kittahngdah]
grocery	a mercearia	er merrsererreeer
hairdresser's	o cabeleireiro	oo kerbherlayrayroo
hardware store	a loja de ferragens [ferramentas]	er lozher der ferrah-zhayngsh [fehrrahmayngtahss]
hospital	o hospital	oo ospittahl
jeweller's	a joalharia	er zhwerlyerreeer
laundry	a lavandaria	er lervahngderreeer
liquor store	a loja de vinhos e licores	er lozher der veenyoosh er likkoarersh
market	o mercado	oo merrkahdhoo
news-stand	o quiosque [a banca] de jornais	oo kyoshker [ah bahngkah] der zhoornighsh
optician	o oculista	oo okkooleeshter
pastry shop	a pastelaria	er pershterlerreeer
photo shop	a loja de fotografias [de artigos fotográficos]	er lozher der footoograh-feeersh [der ahrteegoass foatoagrahfikkoass]
police station	o posto de polícia [distrito policial]	oo poashtoo der pooleessyer [distrittoa poalissyahl]
post-office	o correio	oo koorrayoo
shirtmaker's	a camisaria	er kermizzerreeer
shoemaker's (repairs)	o sapateiro	oo sepertayroo
shoe shop	a sapataria	er serperterreeer
souvenir shop	a loja de lembranças	er lozher der layngbrahngsersh
sporting goods shop	a casa de artigos de desporto [esportivos]	er kahzer der errteegoosh der dershpoartoo [aysporteevoass]
stationer's	a papelaria	er perperlerreeer
supermarket	o supermercado	oo sooperrmerrkahdhoo
tailor's	a alfaiataria	er ahlfigherterreeer
tobacconist's	a tabacaria	er terbherkerreeer
toy shop	a loja de brinquedos	er lozher der breengkaydhoosh
travel agent	a agência de viagens	er erzhayngsyer der vyahzhayngsh
veterinarian	o veterinário	oo verterrinnahryoo
watchmaker's	o relojoeiro	oo rerloozhwayroo
wine merchant	o comerciante de vinhos	oo koomerrsyahngter der veenyoosh

SHOPPING GUIDE

General expressions

Here are some expressions which will be useful to you when you're out shopping:

Where?

Where's a good...?	**Onde há um bom/ uma boa ..?**	awngder ah oong bawng/ oomer boaer
Where can I find a...?	**Onde posso encontrar um...?**	awngder possoo ayngkawngtrahr oong
Where do they sell...?	**Onde vendem...?**	awngder vayngdayng
Can you recommend an inexpensive...?	**Pode aconselhar-me um... barato?**	podher erkawngserlyahr mer oong...berrahtoo
Where's the main shopping area?	**Onde é a Baixa [o centro comercial]**	awngder eh er bighsher [oo sayngtroa koamehr-syahl]
How far is it from here?	**A que distância fica daqui?**	er ker dishtahngsyer feeker derkee
How do I get there?	**Como vou para lá?**	koamoo voa perrer lah

Service

Can you help me?	**Pode ajudar-me?**	podher erzhoodahahr mer
I'm just looking around.	**Estou a ver [Estou olhando].**	ishtoa er vayr [istoa olyahngdoa]
I want...	**Quero comprar...**	kehroo kawngprahr
Do you have any...?	**Tem um/uma...?**	tayng oong/oomer

That one

Can you show me...?	**Pode mostrar- -me...?**	podher mooshtrahr mer
that/those	**aquele/aqueles**	erkayler/erkaylersh
the one in the window/in the display case	**aquele da montra [vitrine]/do mostruário**	erkayler der mawngtrer [vitreenee]/doo mooshtrwahryoo
It's over there.	**Está ali.**	ishtah erlee

Defining the article

I'd like a...one.	**Queria um..**	kerreeer oong
It must be...	**Deve ser...**	dehver sayr
big	**grande**	grahngder
cheap	**barato**	berrahtoo
dark	**escuro**	ishkooroo
good	**bom**	bawng
heavy	**pesado**	perzahdhoo
large	**grande**	grahngder
light (weight)	**leve**	lehver
light (colour)	**claro**	klahroo
oval	**oval**	ovvahl
rectangular	**rectangular**	rehtahnggoolahr
round	**redondo**	rerdawngdoo
small	**pequeno**	perkehnoo
square	**quadrado**	kwerdrahdhoo
I don't want anything too expensive.	**Não quero nada muito caro.**	nahngʷ kehroo nahdher moongʸtoo kahroo

Preference

Can you show me some more?	**Pode mostrar-me mais alguns?**	podher mooshtrahr mer mighsh ahlgoongsh
Haven't you anything...?	**Não tem nada...?**	nahngʷ tayng nahdher
cheaper/better	**mais barato/melhor**	mighsh berrahtoo/merlyor
larger/smaller	**maior/mais pequeno [menor]**	mighor/mighsh perkehnoo [mehnor]

How much?

How much is this?	**Quanto custa isto?**	kwahngtoo kooshter ishtoo
I don't understand.	**Não compreendo [Não entendo].**	nahngʷ kawngprerayngdoo [nahngʷ ayngtayngdoa]
Please write it down.	**Escreva-mo [Pode escrevê-lo], por favor.**	ishkrerver moo [podhee iskrayvay loa] poor fervoar
I don't want to spend more than...escudos/cruzeiros.	**Não quero gastar mais que...escudos/cruzeiros**	nahngʷ kehroo gershtahr mighsh ker...ishkoodhoosh/kroozehroosh

FOR COLOURS, see page 113

SHOPPING GUIDE

Decision

That's just what I want.	**É exactamente o que quero.**	eh izahter**mayng**ter oo ker **keh**roo
It's not quite what I want.	**Não é bem o que quero.**	nahng^w eh bayng oo ker **keh**roo
No, I don't like it.	**Não, não gosto.**	nahng^w nahng^w **gosh**too
I'll take it.	**Levo este.**	**leh**voo **aysh**ter

Ordering

Can you order it for me?	**É possível encomendar?**	eh poo**ssee**vehl ayngkoomayng**dahr**
How long will it take?	**Quanto tempo demora?**	**kwahng**too **tayng**poo der**mor**rer

Delivery

I'll take it with me.	**Levo-o comigo.**	**leh**voo oo koo**mee**goo
Deliver it to the... Hotel.	**Mande entregar ao Hotel...**	**mahng**der ayngtrer**gahr** ow ot**tehl**
Please send it to this address.	**É para mandar a esta morada [este endereço], por favor.**	eh **per**rer mahng**dahr** er **ehsh**ter moo**rah**dher [**aysh**tee ayngday**rays**soa] poor fer**voar**
Will I have any difficulty with the customs?	**Terei alguma dificuldade com a alfândega?**	ter**ray** ahl**goo**mer diffik**kool**dahdher kawng er ahl**fahng**derger

Paying

How much is it?	**Quanto é?**	**kwahng**too eh
Can I pay by cheque?	**Posso pagar com cheque de viagem?**	**poss**oo per**gahr** kawng **sheh**ker der vyah**zhayng**
Do you accept dollars/pounds/credit cards?	**Aceitam dólares/libras/cartas de crédito?**	ers**say**tahng^w **doll**ahrersh/**lee**brersh/**kahr**tersh der **kreh**dittoo
Haven't you made a mistake in the bill?	**Não se enganou na conta?**	nahng^w ser ayngger**noa** ner **kawng**ter
Will you please wrap it?	**Embrulhe, por favor.**	ayng**broo**lyer poor fer**voar**

Anything else?

No, thanks, that's all.	**Não obrigado, mais nada.**	nahng^w oobriggahdoo mighsh nahdher
Yes, I want...	**Sim, quero...**	seeng kehroo
Thank you. Good-bye.	**Obrigado. Adeus* [Até logo].**	oobriggahdoo. erdhehoosh [ahteh loggoa]

Dissatisfied

Can you please exchange this?	**Pode trocar-me isto, faz favor?**	podher trookahr mer ishtoo fash fervoar
I want to return this.	**Queria devolver isto.**	kerreeer dervolvayr ishtoo
I'd like a refund. Here's the receipt.	**Queria o reembolso. Aqui está o recibo.**	kerreeer oo rerayngboalsoo. erkee ishtah oo rersseebhoo

---

Posso ajudá-lo/la?	Can I help you?
Que deseja?	What would you like?
Que...deseja?	What...would you like?
cor/forma qualidade/quantidade	colour/shape quality/quantity
Lamento, mas não temos.	I'm sorry, we haven't any.
O artigo está esgotado.	We're out of stock.
Deseja que o encomende?	Shall we order it for you?
Leva-o ou quer que lhe mande a [em] casa/ao hotel?	Will you take it with you or shall we send it?
Mais alguma coisa?	Anything else?
São...escudos [cruzeiros], por favor.	That's...escudos [cruzeiros], please.
A caixa é [está] ali.	The cashier's over there.

SHOPPING GUIDE

Bookshop—Stationer's—News-stand

In Portugal and Brazil, bookshops and stationers are usually separate shops, though the latter will often sell paperbacks. Newspapers and magazines are sold at news-stands.

Where's the nearest...?	Onde fica...mais próximo/próxima?	awngder feeker...mighsh prossimmoo/prossimmer
bookshop	a livraria	er livrerreeer
stationer's	a papelaria	er perpehlerreeer
news-stand	o quiosque [a banca] de jornais	oo kyoshker [ah bahng-kah] der zhoornighsh
Where can I buy an English newspaper?	Onde posso comprar um jornal inglês?	awngder possoo kawng-prahr oong zhoornahl eengglaysh
I want to buy a/an/some...	Queria comprar...	kerreeer kawngprahr
address book	um livro de [caderninho de] endereços	oong leevroo der [kahdehrneenyoa dee] aynderrayssoosh
ball-point pen	uma esferográfica	oomer ishfehroggrahfikker
book	um livro	oong leevroo
box of paints	uma caixa de tintas	oomer kighsher der teengtersh
carbon paper	papel químico	perpehl keemikkoo
crayons	uns lápis	oongsh lahpish
dictionary Portuguese-English	um dicionário português--inglês	oong dissyoonahryoo portoogaysh eeng-glaysh
drawing paper	papel de desenho	perpehl der derzaynyoo
envelopes	envelopes	ayngverloppersh
eraser	uma borracha	oomer boorrahsher
exercise book	um caderno	oong kerdehrnoo
file	um arquivo	oong erkeevoo
fountain pen	uma caneta de tinta	oomer kernayter der teengter
glue	cola	koller
grammar book	uma gramática	oomer grermahtikker
guide book	um guia	oong geeer
labels	etiquetas	ittikkaytersh
magazine	uma revista	oomer rerveeshter
map	um mapa	oong mahper
of the town	da cidade	der sidahdher
road map of...	das estradas de...	dersh ishtrahdhersh der

newspaper	um jornal	oong zhoornahl
American/ English	americano/ inglês	ermerrikkahnoo/ eengglaysh
notebook	um caderno de apontamentos	oong kerdehrnoo der erpawngtermayngtoosh
note paper	papel de apontamentos	perpehl dee erpawngter-mayngtoosh
paperback	livros de bolso	leevroosh der boalsoo
paper napkins	guardanapos de papel	gwerrdernahpoosh der perpehl
paste	cola	koller
pen	uma caneta	oomer kernayter
pencil	um lápis	oong lahpish
pencil sharpener	um apara-lápis	oong erpahrer lahpish
playing cards	umas cartas de jogar	oomersh kahrtersh der zhoogahr
post cards	uns postais ilustrados	oongsh pooshtighsh illooshtrahdhoosh
refill (for a pen)	uma recarga [carga]	oomer rerkahrger [kahrgah]
rubber	uma borracha	oomer boorrahsher
ruler	uma régua	oomer rehgwer
sketching block	um bloco de desenho	oong blokkoo der derzaynyoo
string	cordel [barbante]	koordehl [bahrbahngtee]
thumbtacks	pioneses	pyoonehzersh
tissue paper	lenços de papel	layngsoosh der perpehl
tracing paper	papel milimétrico	perpehl millimmehtrikkoo
typewriter ribbon	fita para máquina de escrever	feeter perrer mahkinner der ishkrervayr
typing paper	papel de máquina	perpehl dee mahkinner
wrapping paper	papel de embrulho	perpehl der ayngbroolyoo
writing pad	um bloco de escrever	oong blokkoo der ishkrervayr
Where's the guide-books section?	Onde estão os guias?	awngder ishtahng^w oosh geeersh
Where do you keep the English books?	Onde estão os livros inglêses?	awngder ishtahng^w oosh leevroosh eengglayzish

Camping

Here we're concerned with the equipment you may need.

I'd like a/an/some…	Queria…	kerreeer
axe	um machado	oong mershahdhoo
bottle-opener	um abre garrafas [abridor de garrafas]	oong ahbrer gerrahfersh [ahbridoar dee gahrrahfahss]
bucket	um balde	oong bahlder
butane gas	gás Butano	gahs bootahnoo
camp-bed	uma cama de campismo [camping]	oomer kahmer der kahngpeeshmoo [kahngpeeng]
can opener	um abre-latas	oong ahbrer lahtersh
candles	umas velas	oomersh vehlersh
chair	uma cadeira	oomer kerdhayrer
folding chair	cadeira de fechar	kerdhayrer der fershahr
compass	uma bússola	oomer boossooler
corkscrew	um saca-rolhas	oong sahker roalyersh
crockery	louça	loasser
cutlery	cutelaria/talheres	kooterlerreeer/terlyehrersh
deckchair	uma cadeira de repouso	oomer kerdhayrer der rerpoazoo
first-aid kit	uma farmácia portátil	oomer ferrmahssyer portahtil
fishing tackle	apetrechos de pesca	erpertrehshoosh der pehshker
flashlight	uma pilha eléctrica [lanterna]	oomer peelyer illehtrikker [lahngtehrnah]
frying pan	uma frigideira	oomer frizhidhayrer
hammer	um martelo	oong mertehloo
hammock	uma cama de rede [rede]	oomer kahmer der raydher [raydhee]
ice-bag	um saco para gelo	oong sahkoo perrer zhayloo
kerosene	petróleo [querosene]	pertrollyoo [kayrozzaynee]
kettle	uma chaleira	oomer sherlayrer
lamp	uma lâmpada	oomer lahngperdher
lantern	uma lanterna	oomer lahngtehrner
matches	fósforos	fosfooroosh
mattress	um colchão	oong koolshahng͠
methylated spirits	álcool desnaturado	ahlkoool derzhnertoorahdhoo

mosquito net	**uma rede mosquiteira [um mosquiteiro]**	oomer raydher mooshkittayrer [oong moskittayroa]
pan	**uma caçarola [panela]**	oomer kerserroller [pahnehlah]
paraffin	**petróleo [querosene]**	pertrollyoo [kayrrozzaynee]
penknife	**um canivete**	oong kernivehter
picnic case	**um cesto para pique-nique**	oong sayshtoo perrer piknik
primus stove	**um fogão a petróleo**	oong foogahng^w er pertrollyoo
rope	**uma corda**	oomer korder
scissors	**uma tesoura**	oomer terzoarrer
screwdriver	**uma chave de parafusos**	oomer shahver der perrerfoozoosh
sleeping bag	**um saco de dormir**	oong sahkoo der doormeer
stove	**um fogão**	oong foogahng^w
table	**uma mesa**	oomer mayzer
folding table	**mesa de fechar**	mayzer der fershahr
tent	**uma tenda**	oomer tayngder
tent-peg	**uma estaca**	oomer ishtahker
tent-pole	**um mastro de tenda**	oong mahshtroo der tayngder
thermos flask	**uma garrafa termos**	oomer gerrahfer tehrmoosh
tin-opener	**um abre-latas**	oong ahbrer lahtersh
torch	**uma lâmpada de bolso**	oomer lahngperdher der boalsoo
water carrier	**um balde para a água**	oong bahlder perrer er ahgwer
wood alcohol	**álcool desnaturado**	ahlkool derzhnertoorahdhop

SHOPPING GUIDE

Crockery

cups	**umas chávenas [xícaras]**	oomersh shahvernersh [sheekahrahss]
food box	**uma caixa para guardar comida**	pomer kighsher perrer gwerdahr koomeedher
plates	**uns pratos**	oongsh prahtoosh

Cutlery

forks	**uns garfos**	oongsh gahrfoosh
knives	**umas facas**	oomersh fahkersh
spoons	**umas colheres**	oomersh koolyehrersh

Chemist's—Drugstore

Portuguese chemists' don't normally stock the great range of goods you'd find in Britain or the U.S., for example photographic equipment or books. And for perfume, makeup, etc., you must go to a *perfumaria* (perrfoomer-**ree**er).

This section has been divided into two parts:

1. Pharmaceutical—medicine, first-aid, etc.
2. Toiletry—toilet articles, cosmetics.

General

Where's the nearest (all-night) chemist's?	**Onde fica a far-mácia (de serviço) mais próxima?**	awng der **fee**ker er ferr**mah**ssyer (der serr**vee**ssoo) mighsh **pross**immer
What time does the chemist's open/close?	**A que horas abre/fecha a farmácia?**	er ker **orre**rsh **ahb**rer/ **feh**sher er ferr**mah**ssyer

Part 1—Pharmaceutical

I want something for...	**Quero qualquer coisa para...**	**keh**roo kwahl**kehr kawng**ʸzer **perr**er
a cold	**a constipação [o resfriado]**	er kawngshtipperr**ssahng**ʷ [oo raysfry**ah**doa]
a cough	**a tosse**	er **toss**er
hay fever	**a febre dos fenos**	er **fehb**rer doosh **feh**noosh
a hangover	**a ressaca**	er rerr**sah**ker
sunburn	**a insolação**	er eengsooler**ssahng**ʷ
travel sickness	**enjoo de viagem**	ayng**zhoa**oo der **vyah**zhayng
an upset stomach	**indisposição de estômago**	eengdispoozi**ssahng**ʷ der ish**toa**mergoo
Can you make up this prescription for me?	**Pode aviar [avaliar] esta receita?**	**podh**er erv**yahr** [ahvah**lyahr**] **ehsh**ter rerr**say**ter
Shall I wait?	**Tenho de [que] esperar?**	**teh**nyoo der [kee] ishperr**ahr**
When shall I come back?	**A que horas devo voltar?**	eh ker **orre**rsh **day**voo voal**tahr**
Can I get it without a prescription?	**É preciso receita médica?**	eh prerr**see**zoo rerr**say**ter **meh**dikker

FOR DOCTOR, see page 162

Can I have a/an/ some...?	Pode dar-me...?	podher dahr mer
antiseptic cream	um creme antiséptico	oong krehmer ahngtissehtikkoo
aspirins	umas aspirinas	oomersh ershpirreenersh
bandage	uma ligadura [atadura]	oomer liggerdhoorer [ahtahdhoorah]
Band-aids	uns pensos [bandaids]	oongsh payngsoosh [bahngdaydss]
contraceptives	contraceptivos	kawngtrersehteevoosh
corn plasters	pensos para os calos	payngsoosh perrer oosh kahloosh
cotton wool	algodão	ahlgoodhahngw
cough drops	gotas para a tosse	goatersh perrer er tosser
diabetic lozenges	pastilhas para diabéticos	pershteelyersh perrer dyerbehtikkosh
disinfectant	um desinfectante	oong derzeengfehtahngter
ear drops	gotas para os ouvidos	goatersh perrer oosh oaveedhoosh
Elastoplast	adesivo [esparadrapo]	erderzeevoo [ayspah-rahdrahpoa]
eye drops	gotas para os olhos	goatersh perrer oosh ollyoosh
gargle	um gargarejo	oong gerrgerrayzhoo
gauze	gaze	gahzer
insect repellent	uma loção contra insectos	oomer loossahngw kawngtrer eengsehtoosh
iodine	tintura de iodo	teengtoorer der yoadhoo
laxative	um laxativo	oong lersherteevoo
lint	gaze	gahzer
sanitary napkins	toalhas higiénicas	tooahlyersh izhyehnik-kersh
sleeping pills	uns soníferos	oongsh sooneeferroosh
stomach pills	pastilhas para o estômago	pershteelyersh perrer oo ishtoamergoo
surgical dressing	pensos cirúrgicos	payngsoosh sirroorzhik-koosh
throat lozenges	pastilhas para a garganta	pershteelyersh perrer er gergahngter
tranquillizer	um calmante	oong kahlmahngter

SHOPPING GUIDE

VENENO POISON!
USO EXTERNO FOR EXTERNAL USE ONLY

Part 2—Toiletry

I'd like a/an/some...	Queria...	kerreeer
acne cream	um creme contra o acne	oong **krehmer** kawngtrer oo ahkner
after-shave lotion	uma loção para depois da barba	oomer loossahng^w perrer derpawng^ysh der bahrber
astringent	um adstringente	oong erdshtreengzhayngter
bath salts	sais de banho	sighsh der bahnyoo
cologne	água de colónia	ahgwer der koolonyer
cream	um creme	oong **krehmer**
cleansing cream	creme de limpeza	krehmer der leengpayzer
foundation cream	creme de base	krehmer der bahzer
moisturising cream	creme hidratante	krehmer idrertahngter
night cream	creme de noite	krehmer der nawng^yter
cuticle remover	creme para as cutículas	krehmer perrer ersh kooteekoolersh
deodorant	um desodorizante [desodorante]	oong derzoodhoori-zahngter [dayzoadhoa-rahngter]
emery board	uma lima de cartão [lixa de unhas]	oomer **leem**er der ker-tahng^w [leeshah der oonyahss]
eye liner	«eye liner»	«eye liner»
eye pencil	um lápis para os olhos	oong lahpish perrer oosh ollyoosh
eye shadow	uma sombra para os os olhos	oomer sawngbrer perrer oosh ollyoosh
face powder	pó para a cara [o rosto]	po perrer er kahrer [oo roastoa]
foot cream	creme para os pés	krehmer perrer oosh pehsh
hand cream/lotion	creme/loção para as mãos	krehmer/loossahng^w perrer ersh **mahng^w**sh
lipsalve	manteiga de cacau	mahngtayger der kerkow
lipstick	um baton	oong bahtawng
make-up remover pads	pensos de limpeza da maquillage	payngsoosh der leeng-payzer der mahkyahzher
mascara	rímel	reemehl
nail clippers	alicate de unhas	erlikahter der oonyersh
nail file	uma lima [lixa] de unhas	oomer leemer [leeshah] der oonyersh
nail polish	um verniz [esmalte] de unhas	oong verrneesh [izmahl-tee] der oonyersh

nail polish remover	acetona [removedor de esmalte]	erssertonner [rehmoaveh-dhoar dee izmahltee]
nail scissors	tesoura de unhas	terzoarer der oonyersh
perfume	um perfume	oong perrfoomer
powder	pó	po
safety pins	uns alfinetes de segurança	oongsh ahlfinnaytersh der sergoorahngser
shampoo	um champô [shampoo]	oong shahngpoa [shahngpoo]
shaving brush	um pincel para a barba	oong peengsehl perrer er bahrber
shaving cream	creme para a barba	krehmer perrer er bahrber
shaving soap	sabão de barba	serbahngᵂ der bahrber
soap	sabão	serbahngᵂ
sun-tan oil	óleo para bronzear	ollyoo perrer brawngzyahr
talcum powder	pó de talco [talco]	po der tahlkoo [tahlkoa]
tissues	lenços de papel	layngsoosh der perpehl
toilet paper	papel higiénico	perpehl izhyehnikkoo
toothbrush	uma escova de dentes	oomer ishkoaver der dayngtersh
toothpaste	uma pasta de dentes	oomer pahshter der dayngtersh
tweezers	uma pinça	oomer peengser

For your hair

bobby pins	uns ganchos	oongsh gahngshoosh
brush	uma escova	oomer ishkoaver
colouring	um colorante	oong kooloorahngter
comb	um pente	oong payngter
curlers	uns rolos	oongsh roaloosh
dye	tinta	teengter
pins	uns ganchos	oongsh gahngshoosh
setting lotion	um fixador	oong fikserdhoar
spray	laca [laquê]	lahker [lahkay]
tint	tintura	teengtoorer

For the baby

bib	um babeiro [babador]	oong berbhayroo [bahbahdoar]
dummy (pacifier)	uma chupeta	oomer shoopayter
nappies (diapers)	umas fraldas	oomersh frahldersh
nappy pins	alfinetes de segurança	ahlfinnaytersh der sergoorahngser
plastic pants	cuecas [calças] de plástico	kwehkersh [kahlsahss] der plahshtikkoo

Clothing

If you want to buy something specific, prepare yourself in advance. Look at the list of clothing on page 117. Get some idea of the colour, material and size you want. They're all listed on the next few pages.

SHOPPING GUIDE

General

I'd like...	**Queria...**	kerreeer
I want... for a 10 years old boy.	**Quero... para um menino de 10 anos.**	kehroo...perrer oong merneenoo der 10 ahnoosh
I want something like this.	**Quero qualquer coisa deste género.**	kehroo kwahlkehr kawngᵛzer dayshter zhehnerroo
I like the one in the window	**Gosto do que está na montra [vitrine].**	goshtoo doo ker ishtah ner mawngtrer [vitreenee]
How much is that per metre?	**A como [quanto] é o metro?**	er koamoo [kwahngtoa] eh oo mehtroo

1 centimetre = 0.39 in.	1 inch = 2,54 cm.
1 metre = 39.37 in.	1 foot = 30,5 cm.
10 metres = 32.81 ft.	1 yard = 0,91 m.

Colour

I want something in...	**Quero qualquer coisa em...**	kehroo kwahlkehr kawngᵛzer ayng
I want a darker shade.	**Queria um tom mais escuro.**	kerreeer oong tawng mighsh ishkooroo
I want something to match this.	**Quero uma coisa que condiga.***	kehroo oomer kawngᵛzer ker kawngdeeger
I don't like the colour.	**Não gosto da cor.**	nahngʷ goshtoo der koar

* In Brazil: ... **que combine com isto** (ki kawng**bee**nee kawng **is**toa).

beige	**beige**	behzher
black	**preto**	praytoo
blue	**azul**	erzool
brown	**castanho**	kershtahnyoo
	[marrom]	**[mahrrawng]**
cream	**creme**	krehmer
crimson	**encarnado**	ayngkerrnahdhoo
emerald	**esmeralda**	ishmerrahder
fawn	**castanho claro**	kershtahnyoo klahroo
golden	**dourado**	doarahdhoo
green	**verde**	vayrder
grey	**cinzento**	seengzayngtoo
mauve	**violeta**	vyoolayter
orange	**laranja**	lerrahngzher
pink	**rosa**	rozzer
purple	**púrpura**	poorpoorer
red	**encarnado**	ayngkerrnahdhoo
	[vermelho]	**[vayrmaylyoa]**
silver	**prateado**	prahtyahdhoo
white	**branco**	brahngkoo
yellow	**amarelo**	ermerrehloo

às riscas
(ersh **reesh**kersh)

às bolas
(ersh **boll**ersh)

aos quadrados
(owsh kwerdrah**doosh**)

estampado
(ishtahng**pah**doo)

Material

Do you have anything in…?	**Tem alguma coisa em…?**	tayng ahl**goo**mer **kawng**ᵛzer ayng
Is that imported?	**É importado?**	eh eengpoor**tah**dhoo
hand-made	**à mão**	er mahng**ʷ**
made here	**aqui**	er**kee**
I want something thinner.	**Quero uma coisa mais fina.**	**keh**roo oomer **kawng**ᵛzer mighsh **fee**ner
Do you have any better quality?	**Tem melhor qualidade?**	tayng mer**lyor** kwerli**dhah**dher

What's it made of?	**De que é feito?**	der ker eh **fay**too

It may be ...

cambric	**cambraia**	kahng**brigh**er
camel hair	**pelo de camelo**	**pay**loo der ker**may**loo
chiffon	**chiffon**	shi**ffawng**
cotton	**algodão**	ahlgood**hahng**ʷ
crepe	**crepe**	**kreh**per
denim	**sarja de algodão**	**sahr**zher der ahlgoo-**dhahng**
felt	**feltro**	**fayl**troo
flannel	**flanela**	fler**neh**ler
gabardine	**gabardine**	gerberr**dee**ner
lace	**renda**	**rayng**der
leather	**couro**	**koa**roo
linen	**linho**	**lee**nyoo
pique	**piqué**	pi**keh**
poplin	**popelina**	popper**lee**ner
rayon	**rayon**	ra**yawng**
satin	**cetim**	ser**teeng**
serge	**sarja [denim]**	**sahr**zher [**deh**neeng]
silk	**seda**	**say**dher
suede	**camurça**	ker**moor**ser
taffeta	**tafetá**	tahfer**tah**
terrycloth	**turco**	**toor**koo
tulle	**tule**	**too**ler
tweed	**lã tweed [tweed]**	lahng tweed [tweed]
velvet	**veludo**	ver**loo**dhoo
wool	**lã**	lahng
worsted	**estambre [worsted]**	ish**tahng**brer [worsted]
synthetic	**sintético**	seeng**teh**tikkoo
wash and wear	**não se passa a ferro**	nahngʷ ser **pah**sser er **feh**rroo
wrinkle-resistant	**inrugável [não amarrota]**	eengroo**gah**vehl [nahngʷ ahmahr**rott**ah]

Size

My size is 38.	**Tenho o tamanho 38.**	**tay**nyoo oo ter**mah**nyoo 38
Could you measure me?	**Pode tirar-me as medidas?**	**pod**her tir**rahr** mer ersh merd**hee**dhersh
I don't know the Portuguese/ Brazilian sizes	**Não conheço as medidas portuguesas/ brasileiras**	nahngʷ koonya**yss**oo ersh merd**hee**dhersh poor**too**gay**zersh**/ brahzee**leh**rah